El Barrio Remembered

A collection of true stories about the son of
Puerto Rican migrants growing up during the
second-generation decade (1962–1972) in
New York City's Spanish Harlem, El Barrio

Victor López

PAGE PUBLISHING, INC.
Conneaut Lake, PA

First originally published by Page Publishing 2021

ISBN 978-1-6624-5808-8 (pbk)
ISBN 978-1-6624-5809-5 (digital)

Printed in the United States of America

To my wonderful parents—Mary C. and Joe "Pepe" López—who, through their constant guidance, sacrifice, and unconditional love, shaped me into the man I am today.

Gracias, mis padres queridos.

To my loving wife, Ruth. Because of your love and support, I am a better educator, father, and grandfather but, most of all, a better person.

Te amo, mi amor.

To Andrea and Ellen for two decades of support and caring.

To all of you raised in the inner cities of this great country of ours, who drank from fire hydrants and played endlessly on asphalt playgrounds. Those that were labeled as poor, but didn't realize it because you were happy. This book is respectfully dedicated.

Contents

Introduction

The purpose of this book is remembrance and education. It is written to recount a golden decade in the history of New York City, from 1962 to 1972, and the lives of those teens growing up during these much simpler times in a neighborhood called Spanish Harlem or, in Spanish, *El Barrio*.

The 1960s and seventies were important years in the life of New York City. Change was in the air throughout the United States and indeed the world. Among those objects of change were racial and gender inequities, as well as everything from music to fashion. A new world was arising and those of us who were teens during these times had a front-row seat to these proceedings whether we wanted it or not. Men such as John F. Kennedy and Martin Luther King were leading the way regarding how we looked at war, violence, and race. Women were finding their voices and through the use of newfound media outlets, these changes now occurred in your living room through the ever-changing medium of television. Yes indeed, the revolution *was* televised as families saw firsthand everything from the Vietnam War to race riots and the blackout. The Beatles arrived and changed life as we knew it. And the music, oh! The music. Artists such as Marvin Gaye, Bob Dylan, and others too many to mention redefined what we listened to. Motown created a vehicle for African Americans to create a new sound and social commentary. "Salsa," a new type of dance music made up of a mélange of Latin rhythms mixed with a New York sound and attitude, was growing in popularity.

These stories will depict some of the personal occurrences that transpired to me and teens like me in my neighborhood, a small patch of cement called East Harlem. El Barrio stretched from 96th Street to 125th Street and Fifth Avenue to the East River. It was the destination for many Hispanic immigrants as early as the 1930s but came to be the favorite destination for those coming from the island of Puerto Rico. These travelers, who were American citizens by birthright, flocked to East Harlem in New York City for the same reasons that millions of immigrants before them had come—they sought better lives, economic opportunity, and advancement for their children, and the American dream.

These stories chronicle a life before cellular phones, the internet, and video games. They delve into how teenagers lived their daily lives, interacted with their parents and other authority figures, and attempted to make their way in a changing world. They speak to young romance, overcoming racism, and how we studied, played, and grew during some of the most turbulent yet beautiful years in memory. Finally, they speak to how teenagers during these times held fast to their customs, beliefs, and language in an ever-changing landscape where they were always trying to fit in while still staying true to their culture and old-world beliefs.

The Three Strike Rule (1962)

Dreams get you started… Discipline keeps you going.

This morning was like no other in recent memory for me. Our move from the Bronx to the East Harlem section of upper Manhattan had gone well and we were now residents of the Franklin Plaza Apartments. This cooperative development stretching from 106th Street to 108th Street and Third Avenue to First Avenue was newly built and my family had managed to acquire a two-bedroom apartment there. My dad had insisted on returning to "El Barrio" from the Bronx after my mother was mugged coming home from work in our supposedly safe neighborhood.

"Twenty years in 'El Barrio' and nothing happened," he said. "We move and look what happens. We are going back to where we know people."

I had been taken out of Joy Town School, a private school in Fordham Hill that catered to gifted students. My parents were paying a lot for my education, but they believed it would give me a good start. I was learning French and part of an advanced reading program that introduced phonics and decoding at an early age. The school also featured the latest in early childhood instruction as well as an Arts and Music Program. My questions about where I would be going to school were answered this day as my mother broke the news to me.

"You start school tomorrow," she said. "You're going to Saint Cecilia's across the street."

I looked at her with a mix of amazement and panic.

A Catholic school, I thought. *I had heard stories about Catholic schools and they weren't good. Beatings, all-day prayers. Wow.* "I thought you said I could stay in Joy Town until June?" I asked.

"Too expensive!" my dad blurted out over his morning coffee. "Besides, it's right across the street and the neighbors all say that it's a good school, good teachers, and strict."

"Besides," Dad continued, "the fifty dollars a month we save will come in handy."

My mom continued to tell me about my placement as I looked out of the window toward the school building. There it was, directly across the street. It was an old building with clearly marked separate entrances for girls and boys.

"They looked at your report cards and have placed you in the fourth grade," Mommy stated.

"But I'm in the third grade," I replied.

"Well, *mijo,* they must think you're smart. We are going shopping for your uniform this afternoon, so be ready. Uniforms too."

I thought, *That can't be good.*

Unlike my previous school, uniforms were mandatory at Saint Cecilia's. They consisted of an ensemble of corduroy. Corduroy pants, maroon in color, followed by a gray corduroy jacket, white shirt, and maroon tie emblazoned with the letters SCS on it. They even suggested shoes which my mother eagerly purchased. Our purchase was complete and the remainder of my day was filled with being "fitted" for the uniform. My mother, being a sewing "wizard," hemmed my pants and jacket sleeves on her Singer sewing machine. I remember how stiff the corduroy felt on my skin.

How could we wear this in the hot months? I thought.

I would soon find answers to this and all my questions.

The next morning, dressed in my complete school uniform, my mom and I headed out. Instead of a direct path across the street, as I had anticipated to the school, we headed west toward Lexington Avenue.

"Where are we going, Mom?" I asked.

"Oh, I forgot to tell you, the students attend mass every day before school. We are going to the church. That's where the entire school meets."

Wait, what? I thought, *The school day begins in church? How does that work?*

"The students attend mass every day from eight o'clock to eight thirty," said Mami. "Then you walk to the school, nice right?"

Bombarded with both new information and new surroundings, I attempted to take it all in, but it was rough. There on 106th Street and Lexington Avenue stood Saint Cecilia's Church, a beautiful, gothic structure that had been a refuge for thousands of immigrant families that had flocked to East Harlem since the 1920s, its doors always open. Students were milling around and I felt eyes on me as my mom asked for Brother McCarthy's class.

Escorting me to my "area," she said, "Okay, *mijo*, have a good day." And proceeded to the train station to head for work.

No long goodbye, no words of encouragement, just bye. I guess she didn't want to embarrass me in front of all the other kids. "Lineup" was begun and we entered the church. I was awed by the immense structure; we had a church in the Bronx growing up but never like this. Saint Cecilia was a large building with an array of statues, candles, and stained glass adding to its allure. The smell of incense filled the air as we walked to our designated seats in silence. *All* classes were separated by gender in school as was the norm here, as the girls were on the left and the boys on the right.

The 8:00 a.m. mass was in Latin, of course, so I was unfamiliar with the proper responses, mouthing some of them so as not to look like a complete heathen. I also followed my fellow students regarding the frequent mass directives of standing, kneeling, and sitting as I was unaware of these as well. When the mass ended, it was now time to walk the two blocks east to school. This was also done in silence under the watchful eyes of the Christian Brothers of Ireland and the Sisters of Mercy. In retrospect, it was some spectacle watching hundreds of children walking to school in such unison and pageantry.

Pretty cool, I thought to myself, feeling more at ease about my new school.

Once inside my new fourth-grade class, Brother McCarthy introduced me as simply the "new boy" to a fairly disinterested reception of looks and smirks. I was directed to take the seat next to "Herman" and did so. Herman was a thin young man with piercing blue eyes and a confident look on his face, which made me feel a bit more comfortable in my new surroundings.

As Brother McCarthy turned to write on the chalkboard, he must have sensed the confusion and shock in me and, leaning over, said, "Don't worry, I'll help you today, be cool."

I smiled and his concern calmed my nerves a bit.

All subjects were taught in the same classroom and I was holding my own. English class went well as I was called upon to read aloud and did so. Reading was stressed at my former school and I was pleased to be able to show the class that I was good at it. Social studies followed; another good subject for me. I was excelling on my first day. Yeah!

"Mathematics next, men," said Brother McCarthy.

This elicited a groan from several students, confusing me for a bit. Math was my weakest subject, but I would power through and then on to lunch. I was halfway through my first day. To my surprise, Brother McCarthy began to pack his textbooks and left the classroom.

Who was the math teacher? I wondered.

He entered the classroom with a John Wayne swagger that silenced an already quiet space. A massive man who looked even larger dressed in the black vestments of an Irish Christian brother. As he had departed, I saw Brother McCarthy whisper to him that he had a "new student." He never even looked at me as he began to write on the board.

Herman had leaned over during the change of period and said, "That's Brother Sheridan, math teacher." And he was going to say more but was cut short by our new teacher barking directives.

"Multiplication quiz today!" shouted Brother Sheridan.

This announcement was met with groans and unified anguish which he stopped just by glaring around the room.

"Same rules as always," he continued, "the three-strikes rule."

Three strikes, I thought. *What was that about?*

Glancing around the room, I could see students visibly shaken, some almost in tears.

What was happening? I thought.

As Brother Sheridan began to write the ten math questions on the board, I leaned over to Herman and stuttered, "Why is everyone so worried? It's just a quiz."

"It's the strap, man," he replied, trying to calm himself as well. "You get more than three answers wrong on the quiz and you get the *strap.*"

Three answers wrong, I thought. *The three-strikes rule, now I understood that part, but a strap? Whoa!*

Before Herman could elaborate, more instructions were presented... "Clear your desks, men. Put a heading on a piece of loose-leaf please."

All students complied as I fumbled to keep up.

The ten math problems on the board were challenging to me and the announcement of a fifteen-minute time period for their completion did not help my situation. Looking around, I could see my classmates working feverishly to complete the work all with somewhat "glazed" looks on their faces. What was it that instilled such fear in their hearts? What was this strap? Brother Sheridan walked around the room like a sentinel patrolling his post. His large shoes echoing his steps on the wooden floorboards. Passing me, I looked up smiling meekly but no response was provided. After the time period, all papers were collected and instructions were given to read and complete some textbook work while the quizzes were corrected.

He was correcting the tests in class, I thought, *why?*

At Joy Town, all tests were corrected and results were shared the following day.

Why this way? I pondered. *Soon to find out.*

As Brother Sheridan, red pen in hand, corrected the tests, I felt a nudge to my right arm. It was Herman passing me a note, "dangerous move" I thought, accepting the wrinkled bit of loose-leaf paper like a spy in some movie. Reading it from my lap so as not to draw attention, its contents struck at my very core. "If your name is called out, it means you got more than three wrong," it read, "two shots with the strap." My head was spinning. I thought I had done well but what was this strap that he kept referring to?

Was I going to be hit?

Brother Sheridan arose from his chair and announced in a loud voice, "The following men step outside. Johnson, Alecia, McKenna, and Lopez."

I couldn't believe what I was hearing. It was my first day, I thought. *No breaks for the new kid? Unfair.*

Gazing over to Herman, he began rubbing his hands on his pant thighs. He motioned for me to do the same and I began this exercise too. I later learned that warming of the hands prior to being corporally punished reduced the pain level. Yeah right.

Once outside in the barren hallway, all students were "rubbing" their hands. Brother Sheridan exited the classroom. From his waist sash, to my amazement and disbelief, he then drew a piece of rubber formed like, well, a strap. Approximately twelve inches long and three to four inches wide, this was the infamous "strap" I had heard so much about. To be used to punish me and my fellow students this day. I later found out that these "tools" were provided to the brothers by the local shoe repair store. This was the rubber used to replace shoe soles; talk about medieval.

Joseph Guzman, a large kid, was the first to extend his hands as if in an effort to get it over with. The sound of rubber striking flesh resonated through the dark hallways, a horrible *slap* then another. To my amazement, I then heard the student say, "Thank you, Brother" and race inside, clutching his hands for dear life. The corporal punishment continued as the next two students received their "shots," all replying "Thank you, Brother" after the deed was done. It was then my turn.

Ashen from fear after what I had witnessed, I blurted out, "Excuse me, Brother, but this is my first day."

"Doesn't matter," he said, "you're here now, rules are rules. Let's go." Motioning me to extend my hands as the others did.

I did so, trembling with raw fear. As he came down upon me, I must have moved slightly allowing him only a partial strike.

Enraged, he bellowed, "Do that again and we double it."

Steadied by his threat and not wanting to "double" my punishment, I held my second hand out, receiving the full extent of the blow. The pain was like no other I had ever experienced. My entire hand was numb and pulsating as tears welled up in my eyes.

Great, I thought. *You going to cry now. What a sissy.*

I remember trying to harness all my courage in an attempt to stop weeping, and I succeeded in wiping away one or two tears before I reentered the room. I knew that all the guys would be judging me regarding my courage under fire, and I didn't want to look like a punk.

Once back at my seat, I continued to rub my hands on my thighs to offset the pain and to my surprise, it worked as the stinging and numbness began to wane.

At lunchtime, Herman and I sat together and talked. He introduced me around as "the new kid" and I felt a bit more at ease. I knew that this would be the beginning of a great friendship. The afternoon classes consisted of a sing-along in the auditorium/cafeteria with Mr. Woodrow, the vocal teacher on piano.

After dismissal and the walk from school across the street, I wondered how I would tell my parents of the day's events when asked. Then it came to me. Tell Mom everything that happened, show her your hands, present your case, and she will no doubt return you to your private school. Yes, this strategy felt right.

When asked about my day, I dramatically went about recounting the horrors I had faced, even acting out the scene for effect and showing my mother my hands, which were totally fine now.

"Why did they hit you? *Por que?*" Mommy asked me, continuing to eat her dinner without looking up.

"Because I got three multiplication questions wrong," I responded.

"Well, you better study your times tables because you're going back tomorrow," she replied.

No discussion, no nothing. I entered my room dismayed at the outcome of my parental discussion, grabbing my math book and beginning to work on my homework. Later, Mom would go over the times tables with me as she would every night from then on, drilling them into my brain. As it happened, that was the first and *last* time I would face the "strap" for math and the "three strikes rule."

"Don't Skate" (1963)

For every good reason there is to lie, there is a better reason to tell the truth.

Living in East Harlem and, more specifically, Franklin Plaza had opened up a new world of experiences for me. With its playground, showers, and basketball courts all within one complex, I could play all day in relative safety. Though we lived in a so-called poor neighborhood, my friends and I considered ourselves fortunate to have this great "oasis" to play in every day. I discovered many pastimes in El Barrio in 1963. Games such as Johnny on the Pony, Freeze Tag, and the ever-popular sidewalk chalkboard game, Skellies, kept us both busy and fit, but the greatest thing I came upon that year may have been roller skating. Indeed, it was only when I moved to Manhattan that I met friends who skated. In the Bronx, we lived on a busy avenue and the idea of skating was frowned upon by local parents, but here, almost all of my newfound friends owned a pair of these gleaming, steel-wheeled shoe attachments that allowed you to "fly" on the sidewalk with them attached to your shoes or sneakers. It was a simple concept really. Two large clamps held the skate to the front of your sneaker while a strap would go around your ankle, anchoring the skate and transforming you from a walker to a skater.

All my new friends had a pair and I wanted them badly.

"Mommy, please," I pleaded daily.

"No!" she would respond. "For what? So you can fall and get hurt? What do you know about skating anyway?"

"I know how," I would say to her almost yelling but not quite loud enough to set back my chances. "I borrow Ivan's all the time," I would echo.

Ivan was one of my new friends in the building. He would let me use his skates from time to time and even provide me some tips on how to maneuver them. With his help, I became pretty good. He also showed me the workings of the valuable skate key tool. This "key" was important as it allowed you to tighten the front clamps of each skate, thereby holding your foot in place. Very important stuff.

"Please, Ma!" The begging continued for two weeks.

Finally, after a stellar report card, no school-related problems, and Saturday chores done to the letter, it was off to Morris Toyland for skates. Yes, Morris Toyland was located on 105th Street and Third Avenue and it was the mecca of all fun stuff in East Harlem. Morris Wittenberg, a small Jewish man, had opened his store in the 1950s and had seen the neighborhood undergo several transformations regarding its population. At times, he would speak about the Irish and Italian families who had lived in the neighborhood prior to us but never in a negative way. He now embraced the Hispanic community and even showed off his Spanish language skills when needed. He was a kind man who even let you "slide" if you were a nickel or a dime short on a purchase. Morris Toyland had everything a kid could want. Rows of bikes and scooters, model trains, and every toy imaginable lined the store shelves. He also carried school supplies which could be purchased for art and social studies projects, notebooks; you name it and Morris had it.

I walked ahead of my mom that day.

"Wait for me, *coño!*" she shouted as we crossed Third Avenue.

I couldn't remember being this excited about anything in recent memory.

My own skates, I thought, *finally*.

Upon entering the store, we found ourselves being served by Morris himself.

"Roller Skates," he cried out as if announcing it to the entire crowded store. "Of course, we have them."

Within a minute, he produced a red box. Opening it, he held up a shiny pair of new skates. My mother grabbed them before me, eyeing them as if knowing what to look for. Rolling her eyes and with a skeptical look, she passed them on to me for further inspection. There they were all right, complete with red straps and, of course, a skate key in the box.

But wait, something was missing, I thought to myself. "Mr. Morris," I said. "I need the big shoe clamps for the front; these only have the small shoe grips in front."

As part of my tutelage, Ivan had warned me that most roller skates did not come with the large clamps, only the smaller front clamps. These smaller clamps did not work with sneakers and the skate would continually fall off. The larger clamps were extra and cost $1.50 more.

Morris, heeding my request, asked his workers about the large clamps who stated, "We ran out, they are coming in next week, the order was delayed."

"They will arrive in a few days," another worker blurted out.

A few days. I tried hard to hide my distress and anguish. *A few days, what did that mean?* I thought. I wanted to skate *now!*

Mom stated, "Okay, I will pay for everything now and you"—motioning to me—"can pick up your clamps next week, my son."

We took the skates and made our way home.

My mother, with very little skating knowledge but lots of common sense and a knowledge of her son, said, "Don't even think of using your shoes with those things. Wait for the big things for your sneakers."

"*Si*, Mama," I said and arriving home, went directly to my room with the skate box pressed under my arm.

In the privacy of my room, I tried on the skates with my Pro-Keds sneakers to no avail. The straps went around my ankle, of course, but the small grips would not hold the front. Even tightening them with the key would not allow the skate to attach firmly.

What agony, I thought. *I have skates but can't use them.*

Time after time, trying to put them on my sneakers failed, so I placed the skate box in my closet, facing the awful "couple of days" wait period. There, I saw the box that held my school shoes. I remember my mother warning, "Don't wear those things with your shoes." It resonated in my head. My Saint Cecilia's shoes cost $11 and were placed back in their box daily. On Sundays, my dad would take out his shoeshine box with rags and *"betun"* or shoe polish and shine his work shoes while showing me how to polish mine. I had learned quickly and also how to put white "polish" around my sneakers to maintain them as well.

The following day was Friday, All Saints' Day, and all Catholic schools were closed. Ivan knocked on my door, his skates slung over his shoulder.

"Let's go, man," he said. "Time to skate."

I had told him I would have my skates today, so my look of disgust confused him.

"I can't, bro," I said with a long face, explaining my dilemma about the clamps and the "wait period" in front of me.

"You can still skate, man. Use your shoes," he bellowed. "I did before I got my clamps. They work with the shoes, grip real good, man."

I admitted that the thought had crossed my mind but my school shoes and against my mother's direct orders, man, that was taking a chance. What a butt whipping from my dad would be had if anything happened to those shoes. For a moment, my mind drifted off. I saw myself gliding around the block on my new skates, returning the smiles of those envious non-skate-owning kids.

"Stop worrying, man," I heard Ivan say, awakening from my daydreaming. "What could happen?"

What indeed.

As if led by some uncontrollable force, there I was in front of my closet looking at both boxes, one containing the new skates and the other my size seven school shoes.

"I'm just going to see," I stated, declaring a sort of "run-through" as I put on one shoe and then placed the roller skate on.

Ivan assisted in tightening the skate with the key and it felt good.

"Perfect," he coaxed as I placed my skate-laden foot on the linoleum floor.

"Yeah, but will they stay on?" I asked, almost wanting the skate to fall off, thereby returning them to the closet.

"Hell yeah," said my friend. "Shake your foot and move around, you'll see you're ready now."

To my surprise, all the foot shaking and one foot apartment skating did not separate the steel skate from my school shoe.

"It's really staying on," I said.

"Told you; grab your stuff and let's get downstairs."

I put my other school shoe on and carried my skates slung over my shoulder downstairs, still unsure about my actions but wanting to roller skate even more than before.

"Now you are ready, my friend. Let's do this," cried Ivan, rallying me to arise.

In the checkerboard area in front of my building, Ivan had helped as I attached both skates to my shoes, tightening them as much as possible.

Tentatively at first, I began to skate, slowly getting myself together. I found myself rolling around the play area, clumsily at first, and then with a bit more grace and confidence. As time went by, I attempted the basketball court and the parking lot. Together with Ivan as my "wingman," the skills improved and saw me increasing my speed with success. I was now a skater. We had races and even attempted jumps to the chagrin of elderly passersby.

Three hours had passed, and I said aloud, "I'm tired, bro, going to head upstairs."

"One more race, Vic," said Ivan. "Let's go down the hill."

The hill, I thought. *Should we press our luck?*

Not wanting the label of "chicken," I skated alongside Ivan to the small hill. It was a small and winding path between buildings three and four with a slight downturn. It wasn't the 103rd Street Hill on Lexington Avenue or the famed Snake Hill in Central Park, but to us kids, it was challenging and descending it with bike or scooter or now skates gave you some bragging points.

As we began our attempt, I found myself going faster, quickly picking up speed. I was trying to stay side by side with Ivan, a more experienced skater; this would prove a mistake. Approaching the bottom of the hill, I realized I would not be able to stop in time. Bracing for a fall the afternoon air was broken by a loud "*snap*" coming from my right foot.

Oh no, I thought, *not the shoe.*

From the seat of my pants, I saw it clearly. The sole of my right shoe had come apart from the leather upper. There, in broad daylight, was my Saint Cecilia's School shoe flapping like some sort of pelican.

"Oh, snap," said Ivan, coming to my aid. "Are you hurt?"

"No," I yelled. "Look at my shoe, man! The skate ripped off my shoe's sole."

Ivan's face turned beet red when he saw what had happened.

"You're in trouble, man," he said.

Only when I sat on a bench did I realize the full extent of the damage. The sole had been ripped off from the front to the middle, looking like a mouth and flapping in the breeze.

"I'm dead," I whispered. "My dad's going to kill me. These cost $11 and school is on Monday."

Limping home with one shoe flapping in the breeze, I became physically ill with fear. Of course, Ivan, my friend, who had provided such encouragement to me to "go ahead and skate" was now nowhere to be found, having gone home himself. I had gone directly against my mother's instructions and orders and would pay for it now. My dad, a patient man who let my mother do most of the child-rearing as he worked eighteen-hour days as a waiter, would be angrier over my lack of respect than the money, but the money was still an issue. I could hear him now, "Do you know how long I have to work to earn $11?" This was bad, very bad. I put the skates away and took out the box where my school shoes were kept. The thought of the shoemaker had crossed my mind but with what money to pay and frankly, this looked unrepairable. For some reason, as if waiting for divine intervention, I placed the ripped shoe neatly in the box next to the good one and closed the lid.

The sound of my mother's key in the door was usually a wonderful one. Mom was home from work and that signified hugs and a warm dinner, but not today.

I can't tell her, I thought. *My sin was too horrid. The realization that her only son had defied her would be too much for her,* I thought.

So I stayed silent. For the next two days, I was in a daze, stumbling around the house in deep denial with mixed feelings of both worry and fear. Several times, Mom had asked me if I was okay and if anything was "bothering" me. I guess I wasn't doing too great a job hiding my guilt and anguish, but I said nothing.

What will you do on Monday, stupid? When it's time for school, the jig will be up, I thought, *then what?*

I didn't have an answer to that scenario, but I couldn't tell Mom, I just couldn't.

Saturday was "*La Marqueta*" day as I was to accompany my mother to the market under the Park Avenue Train Station. *La Marqueta* ran from 111th Street to 116th Street and was the place where people would buy and sell their wares. All things could be purchased there, from clothing to foods to botanica items. If I was good and pushed the shopping cart without griping too much, Mom would buy me a hot dog from inside the market. For some reason, *marqueta* hot dogs tasted better than the street kind. The only better hot dogs were either at Nedick's in the subway or at Nathan's in Coney Island.

To Mom's surprise, I said "no" when asked if I wanted one. This drew a concerned look from her. I was a ravaged soul still clinging to my dark secret. Strangely, that Saturday afternoon, when we returned, my mother declared that she was going out. I found it strange that she did not specify where but had I asked, I probably would have heard something like, "None of your concern," so no questions.

Sunday passed with church services and homework review then to bed. With Mom working in New Jersey, she would be out of the house at five thirty in the morning on weekdays. This left my father with the task of assisting me with prep for school and preparing a small breakfast.

Exiting from my room, I was in full school uniform, except, of course, for my shoes.

"Put your shoes on," my dad demanded. "You'll be late, let's go."

As I hesitated just a bit, Dad arose from the dining table saying, "*Que te pasa, hijo?* Why so slow? I'll get the shoes; what is wrong with you this morning?"

This was it, I thought, *time to pay for your stupidity.*

I closed my eyes as Pop entered my room, returning immediately.

"Here," he said. "Put them on already. Let's go!"

To my amazement, Dad handed me a pair of new Saint Cecilia's shoes. In his haste, my father had not realized that these were new school shoes, but I did and I knew how they had gotten into my closet, it was Mom.

I must have been smiling because my father asked me, "What are you smiling about? I never seen a kid so happy to go to school," he stated as we left the apartment.

Walking to school, my eyes were filled with tears. She had known all along. That little outing she made on Saturday afternoon was to the shoe store to buy another pair of shoes for me. I guess she knew my dad and how he would have reacted.

Wow, I thought. *Mary had saved me yet again; Mom had my back yet again.*

I wouldn't know it that day, but this would not be the last time Mary Lopez would pull her only son out of danger. I couldn't wait to see her that night to apologize formally and say "I'm sorry" to this great lady and hug her saying, "*Gracias, madre querida, gracias.*"

Mr. Breaststroke/
Palisades Park (1964)

Time will inevitably uncover dishonesty; history has no place for it.

Scientists have wondered for decades about when exactly male puberty begins. I am no scientist, but I do know that, for me, puberty began in the sixth grade in 1964. I know this for many reasons; firstly, that year I was moved from the soprano section of the Saint Cecilia's School Glee Club to the alto section due to my voice changing literally overnight. I was also growing like a weed, forcing my hardworking parents to purchase two new school uniforms in that one year. It didn't help my cause that, as a "chubby" kid, my school pants had to be size sixteen husky which cost two dollars more to purchase. "This boy is too fat," my father would declare. "He eats too much, *esta gordo*," he would say to my mother, who, like all moms of that time, confused love with an extra portion of food. Yes, I was changing and among those changes was a new, intense attraction to the opposite sex. I, along with my entire sixth-grade class, discovered girls in 1964.

The year 1964 also marked the year that the Saint Cecilia's Glee Club came into its own, putting together a string of successful concerts that drew citywide attention. At this particular rehearsal, the director, Mr. Woodrow, announced that as a reward, the entire club would be going on an outing to Palisades Park in New Jersey. Everyone was excited as the day approached. Palisades Park had it all—concerts, rides, games, and best of all, the largest swimming pool in the tristate area. This saltwater pool was the main attraction of the park, drawing visitors from the entire country.

Finally, the day arrived and I was fully prepared with my bathing suit and towel in my bag. Of course, my overprotective mother said that I shouldn't go in the pool as I could not swim, but incessant pleading to my dad resulted in my being allowed into the pool but with his stipulation, "only in the shallow end," to which I hurriedly agreed.

There were four busses making the trip that day and I would make it my business to board the bus that Raquel was on. Earlier that week, Raquel had passed me a note during rehearsal, asking if I would sit next to her on the bus ride and I lit up with excitement. Raquel was very pretty with dark hair and cute features. "Yes, I will," I scrawled hastily on the same note, returning it to her and drawing a smile. I told none of my friends about this interlude as I knew several of them liked her also. It felt exhilarating to have this little secret.

The morning of the trip, students began boarding the busses at exactly seven o'clock in the morning and, as planned, I had positioned myself directly behind Raquel on the line for bus number one, feeling confident in our getting to sit together. As I was about to step up to the board, Joseph, a tall eighth-grader from the bass section, cut directly in front of me without any teacher seeing him.

"Hey," I said, "no cutting!"

He looked at me with a scowl and said, "If you tell anyone, you're a dead man."

As he was the largest kid in the glee club and had a reputation for fighting, I shut up and let him in.

Once on the bus, my dilemma worsened as Joseph, or "Big Joe" as he was sometimes referred to, sat himself next to Raquel in the seat I had hoped to occupy. I sat behind the duo next to Joyce who was Raquel's best friend and who obviously knew about her desire to have been seated next to me.

With applause and screams, the busses began rolling toward our destination. It was obvious that Joseph was trying to "rap" to Raquel, engaging her in conversation and smiling. From time to time, she would glance back at me and Joyce with a look of distress on her face as if saying, "Save me please, Victor," but what could I do? This guy almost took up two seats and if I dared challenge him, he would probably "pound" me right there on the bus. Halfway to our destination, I overheard "Big Joe" bragging to Raquel about his athletic prowess. He, of course, was on the basketball team and excelled at it, but this day, he was extolling his prowess as a swimmer, no doubt due in part to our destination.

"I am the swimming champ at the Boy's Club," he announced for all to hear, drawing cheers from his many minions and smirking my way. "I beat all comers this year," he continued.

And now, to my amazement, Raquel was looking extremely interested in him, hanging on to every word. Her look of panic had now been replaced with one of genuine interest.

I had to do something, I thought. She was being taken away from me right before my very eyes.

With no recourse and in an absolute defensive panic, I found myself blurting out loudly, "I was swimming champion in the Bronx for two years straight, I also dive."

Turning his head around and looking me up and down, Joseph replied, "You? I doubt it, dude."

"Yes," I said, continuing my ridiculous charade, "been swimming for about two years now."

"What's your best stroke?" asked Joseph, pressuring me to falter.

"The breaststroke," I replied, having heard this on a recent *Wide World of Sports* episode.

"Wow!" exclaimed Joseph, impressed at both my quick response and swimming knowledge. "That's difficult."

Once fabricated, my lie took on a life of its own with the girls asking me specific questions about my competitive swimming and me lying through my teeth. Inside, I knew this was wrong, but there was no turning back now. I remembered my father's words that one lie always begets another, but here I was with the girls transfixed on me and Joseph sitting quietly. Looking over at Raquel, she seemed extremely interested in this new side of me and smiled at me for the duration of the trip to the park.

Upon our arrival, everyone made a beeline for the pool. Everyone except me and when asked, I said that I was going to wait for my friend John who was on the other bus.

"Okay, see you inside!" shouted Raquel as they made for the pool entrance.

From the outside, I could see how immense the Palisades Park Pool actually was and a shiver ran down my spine.

How was I going to perpetuate this? I thought. *I suck at swimming.*

I pondered not entering the pool at all and just going on the rides as many members were doing, but that would have prompted so many questions from the girls and derision from "Big Joe" who was probably already inside, dying to see my breaststroke and challenge me to a race.

Why couldn't I just shut up? I thought. *No, you had to lie.*

After thirty minutes of pacing, I decided on a plan. I would go into the pool but say that I had just eaten. All kids were familiar with their parents yelling at them to "wait an hour" after eating to swim.

It might work, I thought. *I would then stay in the five feet and splash around with Raquel and Joyce.*

I changed into my swimsuit quickly and found myself poolside as hundreds of people were enjoying the day. As I looked around trying to get a perspective of where I was in this immense area, I looked down and saw the poolside marker delineating ten feet, causing a shudder to, once again, pass through my body. I continued to look for my companions when out of nowhere, I heard Raquel shout, "Get in the water already!" Running toward me while simultaneously pushing me into the water.

Upon entering the frigid water, I sank like a stone. The panic, only a non-swimmer can relate to, overcame me as I inhaled water immediately. Thrashing about, my life passing before my eyes, I was sure of my imminent death as my feet felt the pool bottom when suddenly, a huge hand grabbed my arm and began pulling me to the surface. The familiar orange and green bathing suit and strength of my savior could only mean one thing, a lifeguard.

I grabbed onto the pool's edge, gasping for air as another guard pulled me from the water. As they lay me on my side, I coughed up what seemed like half of the pool water, looking like a freshly caught fish. Opening my eyes a bit, I could see many of my club mates standing around staring and of course, there was Raquel, a quizzical look on her face.

"What happened? I thought you could swim?" she said louder than I would have hoped.

Having no answer to this question and fully humiliated, I arose and walked quickly to the locker room.

After dressing, I made my way as far from the pool area as I could. Meeting my friends, John and Andrew, I recounted my lying spree to them, attempting to unburden myself and find solace. They in turn began to laugh uncontrollably, finding my story hilarious. For the rest of the trip, I would be known as "Mr. Breaststroke" to their delight. I managed to salvage most of the day going on many rides and drowning my sorrows, no pun intended, in cotton candy and other assorted park fare.

When I did see Raquel and Joyce later that day, I said that I experienced "leg cramps" from the cold water, but I don't think they believed me, walking off without a word.

The lying continues, I thought, feeling especially stupid.

Of course, that was nothing compared to the ridicule I faced upon seeing Joseph again. I felt glad that he was graduating soon and I would not have to see him anymore, but for the remainder of the year, I was "Mr. Breaststroke." Of course, I managed to wangle a seat on another bus going home, having learned a valuable lesson about lying and almost paying for it with my life.

The Incident at the Checkerboards (1964)

Never use the sharpness of your tongue on the mother who taught you to speak.

Summer had arrived in East Harlem at last. I had finished the seventh grade in good fashion with a 92 percent average which meant no summer school, hooray. To me, that translated into long days on Wards Island and bus rides on Second Avenue to John Jay pool for swimming with my friends, both male and female. I was almost thirteen years old now and had recently discovered the opposite sex complete with all its confusion and uncertainty.

The summer also meant hanging out in the checkerboard area in Franklin Plaza. The checkerboard was an area directly in front of my building where guys and girls would sit almost every evening to talk and listen to their 45 RPM records on small RCA record players. Every day about 4:00 p.m., you made it to the "checkerboards" to hang out and listen to new songs like "Cool Jerk" and "Shotgun" and even slow jams like "Hypnotized" and "Ooh Baby Baby." Two or three of the kids would bring their record players and small boxes filled with their 45 RPM records and the music just kept coming. Slow songs were popular with my age group because with these songs came an added feature, slow dancing. Slow dancing or "grinding," as it was referred to, was the art of dancing to a slow ballad while "locked' in a very tight embrace. It was a dance where male and female first encountered the opposite sex, and the dance sometimes led to a kiss or "making out' as we referred to it. As a twelve-year-old kid, I was as yet unfamiliar with this ritual but was anxious to learn. Of course, no one danced like this in the checkerboard area in broad daylight. This was done at the frequent neighborhood house parties or hooky parties' small gatherings that occurred when students skipped classes and met at someone's home while their parents were at work, but we still played both fast and slow tunes because they were hits.

This Friday afternoon, the checkerboard area was packed with teens from around the neighborhood. I had gone upstairs at around three to wash up after playing ball all day in White Park. I then changed my tee shirt and my sneakers and was headed downstairs when I heard mom say, "Nene don't forget upstairs at six thirty, no later, six thirty para arriba."

Oh no, I thought, *I had forgotten to speak to my dad.* It was that crazy time of year when daylight savings time was about to start. My pop had always sided with me that, while my curfew was six thirty in the winter with early darkness, I would be allowed to stay out until dark in the summer that meant around seven thirty maybe eight o'clock. "Mami," I pleaded," Papi lets me stay out until dark during the summer, you know that. Everybodys outside and besides, I'm right in front of the building."

"So what," she answered, "tu papa is not here, when he says so then, okay but today six thirty sharp."

My heart dropped. I knew who would be there today—Miriam, the perfect girl. Miriam was the object of every seventh grade boy's affection at Saint Cecilia's School in 1965. She was smart, beautiful, and, lately, for some mysterious reason, had begun speaking to me during lunch hour and after school. Our conversations had gone so well we had exchanged telephone numbers and had indeed spoken on the phone several times. It was during our last phone conversation that she told me that she was going to the "checkerboards" on Friday and asked if I were going. I, of course, said yes. Here I was close to maybe asking this girl out, and I had a curfew.

"I am not going out at all," I said in a bluff that even I didn't believe.

Without so much as looking up from her crocheting mom said, "Suit yourself," so much for that tactic. Our kitchen clock read four thirty as I ran out of apartment 4A and down the stairs. Opening the building door, I could see the area already crowded with teens, music playing. I walked to the checkerboard using my coolest "bop" and greeted everyone with fives or a nod. There she was on a bench looking great, Miriam. As usual, she was surrounded by her entourage of girlfriends, but I only saw her. She wore wrangler jeans cuffed at the calf in a Capri style. A cute cotton top silhouetted a burgeoning body that made my legs weak. Mustering as much "cool" as I could I approached her and her friends saying to her, "hey girl, how you doing?"

"I'm glad you made it Vic," she said. "Sit down," she continued, motioning to a spot directly next to her.

From across the checkerboard, my boy, Robert, smiled as if to provide encouragement and say *yeah*! We had spoken of Miriam, and he knew how much I liked her. The next two hours were magical as kids streamed into the checkerboard area as the music played. As would sometimes happen some teens even danced. The Franklin Plaza rules stated "no dancing," but the security guards knew most of us and didn't mind, as long as nothing got out of hand. Miriam and I were getting along well talking and smiling. At one point, she even leaned over and touched my knee laughing after a joke. *Wow*, I thought; the touch barrier had been broken. Whether on purpose or subliminally, I sat with my back to my building that day adamant about not going up early. What would Mom do when I didn't show up? What was the worst that could happen? At exactly six thirty-five, I found out.

"Victor Antonio!" a shrill voice was heard even above the music and collective din. "Come upstairs, Now!" continued the announcement. I knew that voice, knew it all too well, it was my mother. I was confused as to how Mom managed to find a vantage point for her tirade as our windows faced 106th Street and Third Avenue, the opposite way, but Mom had gone to our neighbor's house with the purpose of shrieking her son's name and call him upstairs. I didn't answer; I wouldn't answer. Maybe she'll tire. Maybe she will go home.

Right. With a calm pitiful look on her face, Miriam, who had been facing my building said quietly, "Vic, I think your mother's calling you." I was frozen with embarrassment and shame. *What do I do? Stay cool man but how?* My mom is yelling out of a fourth floor window!

Attempting damage control and trying to deflect I found myself saying, "My mom, nah! Must be someone else's mother."

"No," said this beautiful creature trying her best to be diplomatic, "I can see her clearly; it's your mom."

Once again, the calm of the evening was broken by my mother's voice, "Súbe Victor, it's late!"

By now, word of my situation had spread throughout the checkerboard area. Low muffled snickering gave way to all out laughter and what we called "snapping" which meant making fun and denigrating someone. My friend Robert's face reflected a painful smile as he tried to somehow commiserate.

"I wasn't going up." I held fast in my spirit. Going upstairs now, with my tail between my legs, would be the utmost embarrassment; nothing would be worse. It was directly after that thought that the worst possible thing did in fact occur. It was then that I heard the familiar sound of my building's front door opening. *No*, I thought. *She wouldn't.* Yes she did. There in all her glory was my mother, Mary Lopez, walking out of our building toward the checkerboard area. As if this was not enough my mother was wearing a "bata" or housecoat bright with colors and white trim. Of course, she had not had time or the inclination to put on shoes deciding to come down in her "chinelas" or house slippers. These backless slippers made an almost "castanet" sound clacking on the cement floor and announcing her approach. Finally, there were the "rollos" or curlers that she wore in her hair this day. During the 50s, 60s, and even the 70s, women prepared for the week by using hair curlers to produce distinct styles and looks. This day, Mom had outdone herself placing no less than fifteen to twenty curlers in her hair for all to see.

I began to hear a chant, softly at first, then ever louder. What were they saying then I heard it clearly. "Early bird, early bird!" Was the cry from the teenage crowd; it grew louder with each utterance and was of course directed at me, "the early bird."

I took a final look at Miriam, who was obviously embarrassed for me, turned and quick stepped toward my building the sound of cynical laughter still ringing in my ears, passing my mother as she continued pointing her finger and chastising me in both English and Spanish.

Letting myself into my apartment, I felt shaken as I attempted to get a handle on what just happened. How could I ever show my face outside again? Gossip or "bochinche" spread quickly in El Barrio even among the teenage set. *I was a laughing stock*, I thought. Thank god we were out of school for the summer as going to classes; after this, would not have been fun. Then there was Miriam, I was making such progress. It would never happen now. Why would she waste her time with a "mama's boy" an "early bird." The silence in the apartment was broken as my mother entered still shouting in both languages about my disrespect and failure to comply with rules. The familiar "wait until your father gets home!" resonated through the house.

I thought to myself, *how could she? How could she keep yelling at me? Couldn't she see how crushed I was?* Overcome with emotion and reeling from anger, I turned to my mother and said the inexcusable, I shouted out, "You know, Ma, sometimes I could kill you!"

As soon as the words exited my mouth, I realized a line had been crossed. We never talked back to our parents. I had marveled at times when I saw children in the street or on the subway disrespecting their parents with backtalk. Not in my family or in any family I knew. When parents spoke, you bowed your head and listened. And, now this, I was immediately contrite and remorseful, but the damage was done. My mother stood there with a look on her face that reflected disbelief and anger. I expected some form of reaction, but none came. No slaps, no crying, nothing. My reaction however was to run into my room and close the door. The apartment was silent for a time. Pressing my ear to the door of my room from time to time, I could hear mom prepping for dinner in the kitchen. The familiar sounds of plates and silverware clanging as usual. Where was the reprisal? Where was the counter attack? As the hours passed, I prepared for the inevitable talk with my dad upon his arrival home. *I would state my case to him*, I thought. He would understand; we had spoken about this before, and he sided with me. Then there was the part where I threaten my birth mother with death, how was I going to explain that away temporary insanity?

With each passing moment, I became more nervous. When would the beating or "pela" in Spanish come? I then ventured into the dining room area using stealth mode. A plate of rice and beans with chicken had been placed on the table. Grabbing it hurriedly, I retreated to my room to dine and watch my favorite TV show "The Wild Wild West."

Having finished my dinner, but still on Mom watch, it was now time for me to shower and get ready for bed. Prepping my pajama bottoms and T-shirt, I spied through the door again for oncoming danger. As it was all clear, I leapt into the bathroom locking the door behind. I pondered the idea of a mom "sneak attack" in the bathroom but found it unlikely with the glass shower door and other deadly possibilities; after all, we weren't filming "Psycho." Nevertheless, taking no chances, I once again peeked out of the door to see where Mom was in the apartment. I heard the living room television on. She was watching her Spanish soap opera or novella; no way was she missing that; all clear, I bounced into my room. Every minute that went by induced less fear and more confidence in me that mom would wait for my father to arrive before confronting me. The coast was clear for now.

Traditionally, Mom would allow me a snack in the evening, and it was now nine forty-five, "snack time." *A glass of milk and some Ring Dings or Oreos would really hit the spot right about now*, I thought but was it worth the risk? Taking a nothing ventured, nothing gained attitude along with just teen stupidity, I entered the kitchen area almost defiantly. Mom was sitting at the dining room table, her hands in her lap. I passed by her chair and got to the fridge. Big mistake because, you see, the kitchens in my development did not have an exit door. Indeed, it was one way in and one way out. Before I could react I sensed someone behind me, it was my mother clutching something in her hand, was it a belt, a stick, no, it was a spatula, a metal spatula the kind one used to flip pancakes, etc., and she was descending on me with it. With the form of a ninja from olden times, she struck down blows upon me. In disbelief, all I felt was pain as she repeated the phrase, "So you want to kill me!" over and over again. She then changed her battle cry to Spanish saying the words, "mata me!" as she continued her onslaught. Once the attack drew blood from my forearm as I tried to defend myself, I thought mom would relent but no, she kept coming at me saying those same phrases.

Somehow, I eventually managed to side step her and run to my room slamming the door closed in fear for my life. Even now through the door, she continued her repetition of her new found phrase "you are going to kill me!" and the translation, "mata me!" She also combined these with several choice Spanish curse words I had almost never heard my mother say.

I was a mess. There was a bit of blood but no gaping wounds. I trembled for some time refusing to believe what had just occurred. I even contemplated blocking my room door with the bureau but knew Mom would not enter; she had made her point.

After some crying, I drifted off to sleep and was awakened by my father entering my room upon his arrival home. He laughed a bit looking at my defensive wounds getting me some alcohol and band aids.

"What happened boy?" he asked, already cognizant of the answer, "Did you really tell your mother that you wanted to kill her? Tu esta Loco?"

Seeing my obvious trauma at both the day's events and my maternal beat down, he hugged me for some time as I cried in his arms. He then shared with me that, even though my mother was a quiet person, she had the heart of a lion. He also said that she would always try to protect me because I was her only "cub." That was why she was so doting and controlling; still he said emphatically, "You never disrespect a lion."

The next day, Pop gathered his family at the dining room table. Weeping, I apologized to my mother. She nodded but extended no hugs or sentiment toward me. She was still really angry and hurt and would need time to forgive her errant son. For my punishment, my father extended my six thirty summer curfew for another two weeks. I didn't complain because I never wanted to see my mother as "the Lion" again.

Hooky Party/Hickey Party (1965)

Young love is wild and outrageous, laughing at moderation and blinding us to common sense.

Lunchtime was great at Saint Cecilia's School because, as in all other American schools, that was where you interacted with other students and found out all of the school gossip regarding boy-girl relationships and upcoming parties.

This day, the news was more discreet as my good friend, John, whispered something in my ear. "I am having a hooky party this Wednesday; three boys and three girls, are you in?"

A hooky party, I thought, *Wow! I had never been to one of those, but I had heard of them. Boys and girls dancing to slow tunes and kissing while all alone without adult supervision.*

For us, the term "hooky party" didn't really fit as our school, Saint Cecilia's, dismissed its students early every Wednesday for released time, thereby allowing public school students to attend Catechism classes.

"Who is going to be there?" I asked.

"Anna, Gigi, and Mildred," John answered in a hushed tone. "They already said yes. It will be you, me, and Ernie," he added. "My mom will be working until 7:00 p.m., man. C'mon, man, we can dance and hang out."

I knew what that "hangout" meant. It meant that the three couples would make out or kiss. I had never really "made out" before but had spoken to my cousin, Norma, about the subject and she had provided me some advice regarding the art of kissing, so my stomach in nervous knots, I answered, "Okay, let's do it."

With Wednesday arriving faster than I thought, I applied extra English Leather Cologne over my entire body and went off to school. We were to meet John on 110th Street where he lived and go up as a group. As I arrived, I greeted the girls who were already there with a smile. I had always liked Mildred but never had the nerve to ask her out. She was blond with dimples and always smelled great as if she had just gotten out of a shower. To my surprise, she grabbed my hand this day and we walked upstairs together, signifying who I would be with at the party. Entering John's house, I could see that he had tried to create a "mood" by lowering the shades and placing a red kerchief over a living room lamp. As my boys "paired off" with the other two young ladies, the slow music began to play. Cautiously, I moved Mildred to the center of the living room and began to slow dance. She felt great in my arms and, once again, smelled like heaven.

We danced for an extended period, our bodies close but not in a "grinding" sense, just swaying to the music very closely. The 45s on the record player came one after another, extending our embrace in dance. As I pulled back a bit to look into Mildred's eyes, it happened, our lips locked into my first kiss. I tried hard to remember my cousin's tutelage and not panic. "Kiss softly," she would tell me and "Be tender. Girls don't like rough guys." My technique seemed to be working as, when our lips parted, Mildred smiled approvingly.

From this vantage point, I could see that my fellow partiers were also involved in kissing their perspective girls and dancing to the slow tunes. After about a half hour of this "petting," as some people referred to it, Mildred asked me to sit on the sofa with her and I did, where the kissing session continued. My cousin Norma and her instructions were still in my brain as she would say, "Remember to keep your hands where the young lady wants them to be. If you stray, she will tell you no; listen to her or it's over." I was definitely on the same page as Mildred and following her lead as I was being gentle and affectionate but not creepy. It was on the sofa that Mildred began kissing my neck softly. We would stop periodically and gaze into each other's eyes as if we were in a movie. It was pretty cool. The other two couples had gone into other rooms, so the living room was all ours. Then without warning, I felt Mildred's breath on my neck, but now I wasn't being kissed, I was being bitten and sucked. I didn't know how to react to this Dracula-type show of affection and also didn't want to curb her enthusiasm, so I said nothing. Wanting to slow dance again to her favorite song that was now playing, she motioned me to stand and I did. To my surprise, she began to "bite" the other side of my neck in a similar fashion and once again, I stayed quiet, not wanting to ruin the mood. After about three hours, it was now nearly four o'clock and time to go home. We walked the girls as far as Third Avenue but no further as they didn't need the gossips on their blocks telling their parents about them being accompanied by boys. Every block in "El Barrio" had a conduit of older women who spent their days resting on their windowsills, looking around for possible "*bochinche*" or gossip and this would have been major news.

The girls now gone, my friends and I began to talk and compare "notes" on our experiences that afternoon, not in graphic detail but just pubescent boy talk.

Suddenly, Ernie, pulling down my collar, said loudly, "Hey, Vic, you've got two hickeys on your neck, bro, one on each side. Whoa!"

John, also looking closely at my neck, chimed in, "Man, it looks like a vampire attack." Laughing uncontrollably.

In full panic mode, I desperately looked for a mirror to survey my damaged neck. It was only when I approached a cigarette machine that I saw my reflected image and the damage Mildred had done to both sides of my neck. There for all to see were two huge hickeys or "*chupones*" in Spanish. Even my school shirt with its high collar could not hide these new red welts on either side of my neck. It seems that in the spur of the moment, Mildred had thought to "mark her territory," namely my neck, and I was too meek and inexperienced to stop her.

This was bad, I thought to myself as I said goodbye to my pals and walked home deep in thought. My first hooky party, a great experience, was now marred by two large red blotches on my neck. Trying to problem solve, I was stumped as to how to remedy this problem. This was May and warm, so turtlenecks and scarves were out of the question. My mom, being the loving yet doting parent she was, never failed to give me a "once-over" every evening, looking at her only son from top to bottom. She even checked my arms as El Barrio was in the middle of a heroin epidemic.

With no other recourse, I decided to confide in the only family member I could, my father. While not being too specific, my dad had had talks with me about topics such as drugs and girls. After all, this was 1965 and there were many things still "unsaid" between children and their parents, but I got the general idea when we spoke and was glad for his input. Dad arrived home from work early that day and I felt this was a good opportunity for us to speak. Instead of trying to explain what had occurred this day, I began by showing him my hickey-riddled neck.

"*Caramba, mijo*," was his response as he smiled at first and then became extremely serious.

This ambivalence confused me even more as I couldn't tell if he was angry or proud of his preteen son's antics. Grabbing my arm, he led me into my parents' bedroom which had always signified the gravest of situations for me. After all, this was where the "*pelas*" and punishments were disseminated. I was asked to sit down on my parent's bed, my father sitting directly next to me.

Placing his arm on my shoulder, he asked, "*Mijo*, did you do anything else?"

"No!" I answered loudly. "A girl and I just kissed for a while, Pop. I swear, that's all."

"Are you sure?" he asked, looking directly in my eyes. "You can tell me, son."

This was another side of my father that I had never seen before. He was always kind and loving, but with work and other things, he had really never sat me down and spoken to me like this before. It felt great to have his full attention even for a situation like this.

After his initial shock at seeing my neck, Pop went on to speak with me about boy-girl stuff with new candor and pathos. The hickeys may have alerted him to the fact that his little boy was growing up and he had to "school" him a bit.

"What happens between two people is secretive," he said. "This," he said, pointing to my recent disfigurement, "is ugly and announces your private business to the entire world."

I told my father everything that had happened that afternoon, leaving nothing out. He smiled at times but never got off the subject of my hideous neck.

"You should have told the young lady to stop," he said but understood my reticence at ruining my first time.

We both then formed a "plan" as to how we would tell Mary Lopez about the hickeys upon her arrival from work. My dad would lead the conversation and he predicted some yelling and even tears which surfaced quickly.

As expected, Mom was very upset but my dad, as my ally and confidant, softened the blow and assured her that we "had spoken" about everything and all was well.

She was still angry as she asked, "Who was the girl?"

To which I replied, "Just a girl from school." Not naming Mildred as that would have surely ended in a catastrophic trip to her house and parental confrontation.

My dad and my mom also spoke privately where he assured his wife that their only son had only engaged in kissing and nothing else.

That night, my mother took a washcloth and scrubbed her son's neck raw to no avail. It took almost a week for the hickeys to go away even with the nightly Vicks VapoRub treatments Mom provided.

No more neck sucking for me, I thought.

Embarrassment on the
Number Six Train (1966)

Vanity can overtake wisdom; it usually overtakes common sense.

The year 1966 was a year of great change in my young life. I would be attending Power Memorial Academy, a Catholic high school with a rich tradition of both academic and sports excellence. As she was prone to do, my overprotective mother Mary Lopez, conducted no fewer than two "dry runs" that summer of my subway commute to school. Power was located on the west side of Manhattan, several train rides from our home in East Harlem.

"I want to make sure you don't get lost," she would say.

"How can he get lost?" my father would reply. "He speaks English."

Nonetheless, we rehearsed; 103rd Street and Lexington to 59th Street, then downstairs to the number seven train to 57th Street, then walk to school. To be honest, I was secretly glad that we did the "dry runs" as my experience with the NYC subway system was limited and I could use the help.

Riding the NYC subway system was a daily adventure. All kinds of people going places, work, school; it was very exciting and no two days were alike. I had several friends that also went to Power, so we met each morning at the 103rd Street station to travel together.

John, the son of hardworking Italian immigrants, was a good guy. His father owned a building on 107th Street, so he usually had more money that the rest of us and sometimes treated us to pizza and stuff. He was a very intelligent kid who never really studied hard but passed exams with a higher score than the rest of us.

Our morning ritual was always the same. Meet at the 103rd Street candy store owned by Jewish a man called Magish, order a chocolate egg cream or a hot chocolate, depending on the weather outside, and maybe buy a comic book for twelve cents to read later, then the number six train to school.

Fashion played a large role in the sixties and seventies, even in our early teenage lives. Casual wear consisted of woven shirts called "knits" that came in assorted colors and could be purchased at all the men's shops around the city. If you really saved your money, you could then purchase tailor-made pants. This required a trip to "Mr. Tony's" on 125th Street where you created your own pants style. Rear pocket flaps, buttons on the side hem, and specialized waists signaled to onlookers that your slacks were made just for you. Footwear was also a key to "vining" or dressing well. Playboys, a rubber-soled shoe made by a British company, were a favorite. They came in a variety of colors, high top or low tops, leather or suede. You then matched your shoes with your pants and a knit for the complete inner city look. Clean, as we used to say. More expensive shoe alternatives were lizards or gators. These shoes, made of different animal skins, came in full or half designs, were costly and could also be purchased on 125th Street in specialty shoe shops.

The first few days of classes in September 1966 were upon me. I had prepared my school clothes meticulously as Power Memorial required jackets and ties to be worn by all. I would wear one of my two tailor-made pants bought with my summer youth money. I matched them with high-top black playboys, a sport jacket, white shirt, and a tie. Things were looking very positive, but I harbored a secret. A secret that I had succeeded in keeping well-hidden for years that only my parents and some extended family members knew of. I bit my nails. This may sound mundane and even comical, but it was not, I assure you. "Victor," my mother would say daily, "you are going to get an infection, you better stop that." You see, I bit all of my ten digits of fingernails down to the actual cuticle. Due to nerves or who knows what, all were bitten, and I mean raw. I somehow devised mannerisms to hide this disgusting habit from people, especially girls, never extending my hands out or by placing my hands in my pockets. It got so bad that at times, my fingernails would actually bleed. Ugh. "He has to stop this," my doctor would tell my mother at my annual physicals and visits as she tried everything without success. My dad even resorted to corporal punishment, at times whacking me in the hands when he saw me with my fingers in my mouth. Yet it continued as I was unable to stop.

The hours between three o'clock and five o'clock in the afternoon were very special on the NYC northbound Number Six Lexington Avenue subway line. During these magical hours, the trains were crowded with students, included in these groupings were female students returning from their days at such all-girl schools as Cathedral and Central Commercial High School. Students from the local colleges also crowded the cars. Girls from Hunter College and Pace University, to name but a few, crowded the cars, talking and socializing on their way home. These subway cars crowded with high school- and college-age males and females created a kind of "party" atmosphere where grins and looks were exchanged, conversations begun, and maybe, at times, even phone numbers exchanged.

"You got to be cool on the train, man," explained our friend Ray.

Ray was a senior and older than us who, at times, provided advice as to how we should conduct ourselves, especially around girls.

"Don't stare at the chicks, guys," he would repeat. "Don't look so desperate either, just be cool."

At age fourteen, I must admit, I really didn't know what that meant, so I tried to copy what he and the older guys were doing. My friend John was also a novice at this "being cool stuff," so we sat there together as the train came to its best stop, 59th Street, home of Cathedral School for Girls. The doors opened and girls just "poured" into the subway car, resplendent in their blue school uniforms. There were some pretty short skirts on some of these females, I noticed. It was only years later that I was told that some of these young ladies hiked their skirts up at the waist for a cuter effect.

There are so many, I thought. *Blond, brunette, short, and tall with pleated skirts and knee socks, all around us.*

We sat motionless, taking it all in. Ray's words resounded in my brain, "Be cool." I fidgeted in my seat, refusing to make eye contact with anyone except my friend John, who looked just as petrified as me. The subway car now smelled of Jean Nate and Charlie, two popular female fragrances of the day, as the doors closed and the train lurched forward on its way uptown. Suddenly, I remembered a lesson taught to me by my father, "Always give up your seat on a train or bus to a lady, this will make you a *caballero*, a real gentleman."

Wow! I thought to myself. *This will be great; I'll do it and show all these girls that I am a caballero.*

With a big smile, I stood up in the overcrowded train and motioned to the closest schoolgirl to please take my seat. This was met with a smile and the soft "purr" of giggling from her many friends. My boy John smiled as well, envious of my chivalry. Suddenly, the train lurched badly once again and I found myself off balance, almost falling. This would have been catastrophic, the new "cool" guy falling down in the subway car.

Instinctively, I grabbed for the pole. NYC subways cars had silver poles at each end of the car for standing passengers. These were good as several riders could hold on simultaneously and avoid falling. You held on making sure your hand did not touch another person's hand in the process. This unwritten rule of the subways was one of many I had learned. I grabbed the pole and hung on proud of my gallant gesture and newfound notoriety. Then I heard it, girls laughing and giggling softly at first then increasingly louder. I coolly looked around, hoping to see the target of their laughter. Slowly, it became clear to me who the ladies were laughing at, it was me. In the moment of my seat triumph, I had forgotten to hide my hand that was now grabbing the pole for all to see. My nails, eaten away and grotesque, were there in plain sight.

One girl began the verbal assault. "Look at his nails," she squealed in a high-pitched voice. "They look like the 'nubs.'" Using this word, referencing a television commercial that was popular during that period whereby a bad shave was called the "nubs" by women.

Like wildfire, the verbal abuse spread throughout the car. One girl told another and the laughter was crippling to me. Even my so-called boys chimed in with ridicule, saying things like "You should put some gloves on, dude," and "Hey, that's nasty."

My face turned crimson and I felt faint from the verbal assault. Like a wave, people in middle car asked what was so funny and laughed when told about my disfigured hands.

"Eighty-Sixth Street," bellowed the overhead speaker.

The moment the doors opened, I ran out of the car, still able to hear the laughter inside. I stood on the platform stunned at the turn of events, my hands deep in my pockets, the object of finger pointing and continued name-calling. As I waited for another train to ride the two stops north to 103rd Street, my parents' warnings about this very thing echoed inside my brain. Why hadn't I listened? Another parental lesson learned the hard way.

"*Que te paso, mijo?* What happened?" my father asked me, no doubt noticing my ashen color and distressed look.

When I recounted what had happened to me, he burst into laughter. Not the reaction I was expecting. I locked myself in my room, vowing never to leave. After two hours, my mom arrived from work and they both came in and spoke to me.

"We told you to stop biting your nails," said Mommy.

My dad apologized for laughing at me even as a continuous smirk covered his face.

"It's not funny, Pepe," said my mom as she also tried to keep a straight face. "We will help you stop, baby," said Mom. "We promise."

It took a long time and continuous support, but I eventually did stop the nail-biting as each time I was tempted to place my fingers in my mouth, I thought of that train fiasco. By the way, as a precaution, I took the Third Avenue bus home for the next three months as the train was still scary. Just saying.

The Candy Incident (1967)

The excitement of violence exhausts the mind and leaves it withered.

The greatest daily adventure during my entire high school years had to be the train rides to and from school itself. The NYC subways were a reflection of the great melting pot that was New York; all cultures, all races, people from every monetary strata packed into these "tubes" going to and fro, it was crazy and exhilarating. My mother worried about my commute and would always shout warnings at me as I opened the front door to leave.

"Be careful," she would say. "*Hay, muchos locos en el tren.*"

"*Si, mami,*" I used to say as I left, not knowing what surprises would present themselves.

This particular ride home from my beloved Power Memorial was unlike any other in recent memory. For some reason, the Number Six Lexington Avenue line was more crowded than I, or my friends, had ever seen it. It was also June and the temperature in the greatest city in the world had skyrocketed to ninety-three degrees; not the best weather to be underground in a subway car with over a hundred or so people.

"Damn, it's roasting in here, there's no air," said my boy Tommy.

Tommy was one of the real tough guys from 106th Street. He was a member of a large Italian family who refused to relocate from East Harlem as the neighborhood "changed" from Irish and Italian to predominantly Hispanic. He was very strong and good with his hands which he proved on an almost daily basis, refusing to be bullied and picked on by guys from other blocks. As time went on, the entire neighborhood knew and respected this "*Italiano*" as a standup kid who would defend himself and his family.

"I'm dying here!" shouted John, my other Italian friend, sweat pouring from his brow.

As we pulled into the 68th Street station, I noticed Tommy making his way toward the subway's connecting doors. All NYC subway trains were connected by doors at the cars' ends. Riders could travel from car to car by opening these doors and stepping out onto the conductor's platform then reentering another car. During the 1990s, these doors were locked as riders began accessing and exiting the subway via this opening between cars, jumping over the ropes. Tommy opened the car door, motioning for us to follow and we did. We were now riding on the conductor's platform between the subway cars.

"Wow, it's much cooler here," said Tommy.

"You can breathe better too," chimed John. "And no stinky-people smell."

The NYC subways were open to all paying customers and at times, you may have found yourself sitting or standing next to someone who did not share your concepts of personal hygiene and bathing regularly; this made for a long, smelly commute. We were okay now riding home with the underground breeze caressing our faces.

Only four stops to get home. I thought, *103rd Street, here we come.*

As we were being hurled home, we felt fortunate riding between the cars. People looked at us riding in comfort as they were being pressed together like sardines in a can.

"This is the greatest," said Tommy. "Why didn't we think of this sooner?"

"I think it's illegal," I said, trying to sound informative but not scared. "You're not supposed to ride here," I continued, pointing to a sign on the car stating that very fact.

"You always got to ruin things, man," countered John. "Go back into the car if you're scared," he said, challenging me.

"Nah, I'm cool," I replied, mustering my courage as the number six train jolted back and forth.

Riding between the cars, you felt every lurch and movement of the train, much more than riding inside, but I stayed fast, no punking out today. I knew that if I returned to the subway car, the entire neighborhood would know about it by that evening.

"Seventy-Seventh Street," the loudspeaker beckoned.

Great, I thought. *Three stops to go.*

I was conflicted as I traveled that day. I had never done anything illegal in my life and, while this was no bank robbery or major offense, it really wasn't something that I would "ordinarily" do. I was trying to be cool and tough just to fit in. I couldn't shake this sense of foreboding.

Can't wait to get off this train, I thought.

"Watch the closing doors!" crackled that speaker once again and we were off.

It was then that I noticed John eating something, it was candy and he was "sneaking" it into his mouth from his pocket.

Tommy noticed it too and said, "Hey, man, what you eating?"

It was an unwritten rule that if you had candy, chips, or any kind of food, you were supposed to share with your boys.

"M&M's," John stated grudgingly. "I only got a few left," he continued, obviously lying to keep his candy reserves to himself.

"Let me get some!" shouted Tommy above the train noise, holding his large hand out.

John immediately shared some of the colorful candies with him and motioned to me to take some as well, but I nodded no. I loved chocolate but didn't want to chance an acne breakout. At fourteen, chocolate was the enemy of clear skin.

The train pulled into the 86th Street station and people exited. A loud "*hiss*" of the brakes and we were off again. As we slowly left the station and with no warning, Tommy began to hurl his M&M's at the people walking on the platform, striking them with pinpoint accuracy and laughing uncontrollably. Seeing this, John also began pelting the unsuspecting people with the colorful confection, drawing shouts of "Hey!" and "Ow!" from his victims. I, too, got caught up in the moment laughing and egging on my friends.

Entering the tunnel between 86th Street and the upcoming 96th Street stations, Tommy and John began to conspire about their next "candy attack." They would, once again, wait for the doors to close and then hurl their projectiles at the people as they proceeded to the exits. John handed me a handful of the candies so that I could participate in the next onslaught and I reluctantly grabbed them from his chocolate-stained hand. I knew that my participation or lack thereof would be spoken about on the 106th Street playground that very afternoon. As we exited the 96th Street station, my friends, once again, began firing their candy pieces at unsuspecting citizens. Once again, choice expletives were being yelled at us by those being struck. I threw my pieces, but they did not find their mark as I was furthest away from the platform. I also did not aim well, hitting the walls and thinking that these actions were really wrong. Looking into the train car, I could see the anger and disgust of people glaring at us in disbelief. My two friends, however, were really in the moment, slapping each other "fives" and still laughing wildly.

It was then that I perceived something strange in the train car to my left. As if from nowhere, there was a man standing and staring at us, his face almost touching the glass of the connecting door. I could see he was a large man wearing a suit jacket and tie glaring at us with a look of disapproval on his face. Preparing to exit this train at 103rd Street, I turned to the other car, pulling the door latch. To my surprise, here was another huge man directly in front of me.

This man had a gold badge in his hand and barked loudly, "New York City Transit Police, all three of you get off at the next stop!"

Surveying the train, I thought, *Nowhere to run, no place to go.*

Our safe, cool train platform was surrounded as both men stared at us, almost daring us to try and escape. I remember looking at the passengers' smiling faces which reflected relief that we had been stopped.

"One hundred third Street, Lexington Avenue," announced the conductor.

That announcement was usually met with inner joy by me; it meant I was home, my neighborhood, my *barrio*; not today.

As the car doors opened, the two hulking men, transit detectives, I later realized, grabbed all three of us by the collars and escorted us to the platform to the joy and applause of the remaining riders. My friend Tommy seemed unaffected by this sudden turn of events, smirking when asked questions by the cops. Tommy had had brushes with the law before, so this was nothing new to him. John was obviously worried as his normally pale color grew even paler. Like me, he was submissive and silent. Our families were first generation immigrants and criminal acts were not taken lightly. I could hear my father's voice in my head and felt a sudden urge to urinate from fear. I held it because the story of "Victor pissing himself" would not add to my legacy. Well, here we were, we were placed against the wall of the platform and were questioned by the cops, pen and pads in hands, taking copious notes. In hindsight, these veteran policemen probably saw that we were not career criminals, just stupid kids engaging in tomfoolery. The station agent at the 86th Street station had called the police after several commuters had complained of being hit with objects as they exited the train. The police boarded the number six train at 96th Street and observed our crimes firsthand before stopping us.

All of our personal information was taken—names, school, addresses, and parents' names. Of course, Tommy being Tommy tried to provide a false name to the detectives when questioned, forgetting that his real name was scrawled all over his notebook. This further angered the cop questioning him.

Apparently sensing my angst and seeing that I may "pass out," one of the detectives came over to me, and in a quiet voice said, "You all right, kid?"

"Just real scared, sir," I whispered. "I never been in trouble before," I continued, speaking softly so as not to be heard by my confederates. "What's going to happen to us?" I asked naively. "Are we going to jail?"

"Nah!" he said. "But you will have a JD number."

A JD number, I had heard of this. In the 1950s and sixties, all people younger than sixteen years of age caught committing "petty" crimes would be given a "JD card or number." This would serve to identify you to the criminal justice system. It was said that three incidents of this kind would get you into serious legal trouble and identify you as a repeat offender.

The other detective, obviously the "bad cop" in this scenario, chimed in, yelling loudly, "You could have hurt someone, you idiots! There were women and kids on that platform. Your parents will receive notification of your actions by mail." He continued, "Any more of this foolishness and you *will* be arrested; now get out of here and go home!"

The walk home was silent; I believe we were still in shock. Even Tommy, the tough guy, couldn't believe what had just happened.

"I'm done, man," he murmured. "This is my second offense, my mom is going to kill me."

He went on to provide a "tutoring" session on what would happen now. He said that in about two to three weeks, we would receive a manila envelope in the mail with all the information as to what we got caught doing. It would further say that we now had "juvenile delinquent" status and provide our parents with our JD number. After saying our goodbyes, I walked home in a trance of disbelief.

Do I tell my parents or not? I thought.

Not knowing if my highly strung, overprotective mother could bear the strain of her only son being branded a juvenile delinquent, I decided to gamble and stay quiet. My father, who worked nights as a waiter for wages and tips, would certainly react by giving me the beating of my life, no question. He was very proud of his Catholic school son but never spared the rod when an occasion arose. During these times, only the timely intervention of my mother stopped further corporal punishment from occurring.

This was bad, I thought. *Police involvement, letters home, a record. I was also done for.*

Days passed and turned into weeks, still no letter from the transit police. Neither my mother nor father had found it strange that I "volunteered" daily to go to "*el buzon,*" the mailbox, and retrieve the day's mail. Each and every day, I opened that mailbox in search of that manila envelope, but no correspondence.

"Wow," I said to myself after almost four weeks. *Maybe they forgot about it? It was a petty act, not important,* I thought. I felt relieved that there would likely be no letter.

I arrived home at precisely six o'clock in the evening this Saturday, beating the streetlamps to the universal "time to go home" signal in East Harlem and every inner-city neighborhood. Entering the apartment, I knew something was not good. My mother was shaking her head in disapproval from side to side, her eyes glazed over with tears. My dad, Joe "Pepe" Lopez, who had always claimed that he "had never seen the inside of a courtroom or police precinct" with pride, was holding a large manila envelope in his right hand; it had arrived today. Emblazoned on the outside, I could see "New York City Transit Police."

"Why didn't you tell us?" My mom cried out tears streaming from her beautiful brown eyes.

"I was scared!" I replied as I cried that familiar cry children do while attempting to speak and weep simultaneously, gagging on words, snot running from my nose.

In full panic mode, I listened as my father said, *"Lee esto,* read what you did."

Dad seemed strangely calm for the father of a recently specified juvenile delinquent; the bottle of Bacardi and accompanying shot glass on the dining room table spoke volumes regarding his calm demeanor. Handing me the letter, I began to read aloud as he had demanded, every word exacting a sob from my poor mother.

The letter read, in part, "Dear Parent, your son, Victor Lopez, was apprehended riding on the conductor's platform of the Lexington Avenue subway on…"

As I read it, the stupidity in which I had been involved that day finally dawned on me. "Someone could have gotten hurt," the detective's words resonated in my head. He had been right. I had followed my peers, allowing what others would think to take precedent over what was right. I felt totally foolish.

Having finished my allocution, I sat down beside my parents on our sofa, the plastic slipcovers adding to my perspiration, and retold them the entire story, leaving nothing out. Crying uncontrollably, not for just having been caught but for shaming my family, I think they knew my remorse was real.

"*Vamonos para el cuarto*," my father commanded.

"Don't hit him, Pepe, he is sorry," my mom said, pleading for leniency.

I entered my parent's bedroom, quivering and also wondering as to what would be my manner of punishment. The belt maybe or slaps, which we called "*bofetadas*" in Spanish.

"Sit down," my father said, a tired look on his face. Calmly, he stated, "Everyone gets one chance and this is yours," trying in his best broken English to better communicate with his only son. "But I will tell you," he continued, "if anything like this happens again, *yo te mato!*" Which translated was a death threat and not a veiled one, by the look in his eyes.

I was then banished to my room and told to stay there while my parents conferred. Four weeks, a month, that was my sentence for my subway crime. No playing outside, no Boy's Club, no nothing! Home from school at exactly three thirty in the afternoon without fail and I was also told that I needed new friends to which I agreed. In my room, I sat on my bed and sighed, thinking to myself of what could have been my outcome. Four weeks punishment was not a bad sentence for the first and only crime I ever perpetrated.

The Delivery Job (1968)

Prejudice, even when trying to lift your own, is wrong.

All my young life, I had seen my parents' work ethic on display daily. My father, a waiter at a high-end midtown hotel, had worked his way up from dishwasher to busboy to maître d', working sixteen-hour days at times. Mom worked in a factory in New Jersey, making women's handbags six days a week at times. I had reached the age where I wanted my own money so as not to rely on them all the time and to help with the household expenses.

This day, my two friends and I were going to the movies on 86th Street when, as I stared out of the window, I saw a sign in front of Krauss' Bakery that read, "Delivery boy wanted, inquire within." I made no mention of this to my friends but made a mental note that the store was on 90th Street.

Excited, I spoke to my parents that evening about the idea of me getting a job. Of course, Mom was hesitant, but my dad immediately said yes, stating, "He rides his bike all day anyway, might as well get paid for it."

Monday, after school, I hastened to the bakery, wearing my school shirt and tie and confident in my abilities. Krauss' Bakery was located in a neighborhood known as Yorkville and had been a mainstay in that community for decades. As I entered, Mrs. Krauss, a diminutive woman, approached me.

"May I help you, young man?" she asked in an Eastern European accent.

"I am here to apply for the delivery job, ma'am," I said.

"What is your name?" she inquired.

"Victor," I replied politely, making full eye contact and smiling.

"My husband usually takes care of these things," she went on to say. "He will return tomorrow, I am waiting for my daughter to arrive."

As we spoke, customers began to enter the store and produce receipts for their orders to be picked up. A jittery Mrs. Krauss seemed overwhelmed by the rush, so instinctively, I began to assist her. I handed her orders and produced boxes for the pastries and cakes to be packaged, even holding open the door for people entering and exiting the store. As a half hour went by, the rush ebbed. Then Mrs. Krauss' daughter arrived. She must have been nineteen or twenty years old with piercing blue eyes and blond hair.

"Inga, this is Victor," said Mrs. Krauss. "He is here for the delivery job. He was very helpful to me today."

Smiling Inga thanked me for assisting her mother.

"Would you like a pastry?" asked Mrs. Krauss from behind the huge showcase filled with baked delights.

"Yes." I said "Thank you" kindly.

When the demure woman extended her arm to give me my reward, I saw it. On her forearm were numbers, they were tattooed on.

Seeing that I noticed, she stated nobly, "I was in a concentration camp during the war."

Briefly, I recounted to her that I had learned about the holocaust in school and admired her courage and candor.

Looking at Inga, I felt she was a bit embarrassed by this topic as she said, handing me a paper, "Fill out this application and bring it in tomorrow. I will tell my father of your assistance today and thank you once again."

Smiling, I returned home to tell my parents about my interview process. I spoke to them about the "number" incident and even looked up the holocaust in my Britannica Encyclopedia so that they could understand better.

"What terror that woman must have endured," said Mom.

As we read about Hitler and his "Final Solution," I thought to myself that all people had been persecuted at one time or another for many reasons, race, religion, and creed. Will this ever stop?

After my final class on Tuesday, I sprinted to the bakery. Adjusting my coat and tie, I entered the crowded store. There, in the front, was Mr. Krauss. He was well over six feet tall with gaunt features that signified a life of struggle and perseverance.

Greeting me warmly, he said, "You must be Victor, my wife and daughter told me about your assistance yesterday, I appreciate that."

"It was my pleasure, sir," I said as contritely as I could but still making eye contact with a voice of assurance.

I handed him my application and he began to peruse it immediately.

This was it, I thought. *He may want me to start today.*

I had packed a pair of dungarees (jeans for you, younger kids) a tee shirt and sneakers in my gym bag in case I was called to duty today.

Suddenly, the calm of the bakery was shattered by Mr. Krauss. "Victor Lopez! That is your name? Where were you born, son?"

Taken aback by this line of questioning, I said, "In the Bronx, sir, but I live in Manhattan now, on 106th Street and Third Avenue."

"And your parents, where are they from?" he bellowed with a look of disdain on his face.

"The island of Puerto Rico, sir; we are of Puerto Rican descent."

As he handled the application, I could see tattooed numbers on his forearm as well. Mr. Krauss had also been the target of Hitler's hatred, no doubt having also lost family members and loved ones to the Nazis. His demeanor having changed completely and his once smiling face now reflecting a sneer.

He shouted to me, "Did you write your phone number here, young man?"

"Yes, I did, sir," I replied in a low murmur.

"Then I will call you!" With that, he turned and walked toward the rear of the store.

On my way out, Inga entered and greeted me warmly.

"Papa, did you meet Victor?" she said before I could interject a warning as to his mood.

"Yes!" was the father's answer as he summoned her to the rear of the store.

Leaving slowly, I looked toward the rear of the bakery. There I could see Inga and her father in what seemed to be a heated discussion. I knew she was receiving a tongue lashing because, like Hispanic children, her bowed head and submissive manner reflected respect for parents. As I reached the door, Inga appeared in her apron and set about her tasks. As I opened the door to finally leave, she gazed at me with tears in her eyes then looked away.

What had happened? I thought. *What had I done to screw this up so badly?* The bus ride home was filled with many questions and few answers.

As I conveyed the occurrences at the bakery to my parents that evening over dinner, two very different opinions emerged. My mother, ever the optimist, thought that maybe Mr. Krauss had promised the job to someone else, a family member or such and, not having told his wife and daughter about this, he was visibly upset.

"Then why the questions about his parents and where we are from!" shouted Pepe Lopez. "He doesn't want Puerto Ricans working there, plain and simple. *Racismo* just as always."

A week passed and no telephone call from Mr. Krauss.

"They should at least call and tell you that you were not chosen," my mother would say. "At least that."

"They will not call!" stated my dad. "They are cowards; all racists are cowards."

"Calm yourself, Pepe," my mom would say softly. "He will have other opportunities."

Three weeks having gone by and the bakery incident just a memory. I accompanied my mother to Gimbels on 86th Street. She would pick up a suit for me that had been placed on lay away. Lay away was an ingenious manner of shopping that dictated paying for an article "over time" then obtaining it when final payment had been reached.

Peering out onto Lexington Avenue as we passed by 90th Street, my eyes witnessed a curious sight. There, in front of Krauss' Bakery, was a delivery boy locking the delivery bike to a post. He was about my age and my height; on his head he wore a "Yarmulke," a traditional Jewish head covering for men. I immediately drew my mother's attention to this and we both stared at the scene as the bus went on downtown.

It seemed that my dad was correct and Mr. Krauss did want a Jewish youngster for the position. Seeing my look of astonishment, my mother tried to console me. She, and my father, had always regaled me with stories of when they arrived in New York. They included horrible tales of being called "spic," having doors slammed in their faces, and only being able to obtain menial work.

"Mom," I asked, "how did you get through it?"

"You must be the best at anything they ask of you" was her reply. "If you wash dishes, then be the best dishwasher you can be. Then they will see the real you—the dedicated person, a worker, not a name or a skin color."

Her words rang true this day. After all, no one had endured more than the Jewish people and now they were captains of industry yet, still to this day, even they were still the objects of racism.

As I rode the bus next to my mother, I felt a changed person. I thought I was adverse to racism, being White with blondish hair, but my last name had thwarted that. I was Hispanic, a Puerto Rican, and that day, I learned to wear that tradition proudly.

"Should I hate Mr. Krauss, Mom?"

"No, *mijo!*" Mom said loudly. "He was trying to lift his own people just like all races do. Never hate, *papi*, hate eats you up inside." She said lovingly, "You must study, work hard because when you are a success, we all succeed."

From that day on, I walked differently, I spoke differently, and I applied myself to all I did. I can't explain it, but something was triggered inside me. Call it pride, call it will; all I can say is that this Puerto Rican was going to succeed. No doubt for my family, for my heritage, and yes, for my parents who had sacrificed so much for me.

Pilfering at Alexanders
Department Store (1968)

If it's not yours, don't take it. If it's not true, don't say it. If it's not right, don't do it.

Teenage years, whether in an inner city setting or in a rural area, can be challenging and fraught with difficult decisions regarding right and wrong. These daily decisions can also be swayed, at times, by peer pressure or the wanting to fit in with a crowd or group. Nowhere was this more obvious to me than in the year 1968.

At age sixteen and in my junior year of high school, I found myself experiencing more decision making and facing more temptations than ever before in my life. I had successfully managed to stay away from narcotics, namely heroin, as the drug epidemic had ruined the lives of many a friend and family around East Harlem and, indeed, the entire city.

One morning, over breakfast at the Power Memorial cafeteria, I overheard my good friends speaking and boasting about their "free stuff." They went on and on about their new shirts, baseball gloves, ties, and other assorted items they had "acquired." When I inquired as to how they had obtained these newfound items, they smiled and snickered to one another, not saying a word to me.

As they continued and my inquisitiveness got the better of me, I pressed them for answers when finally, my friend Steve said, "You're not made for this, bro, and you don't have the nerve for what we do after school."

This comment elicited laughter from my other East Harlem friends, John and Lenny. As I sat there, my gut told me that my boys were involved in some "shady" activities after school and I should just nod and leave it at that. My father had always told me not to be a follower as most parents did, but here I sat, wanting peer acceptance and approval.

So I took the "bait" and replied, "C'mon, guys! I can hang. What's the deal!"

Looking around mysteriously, Steve said, "Come with us at dismissal, bro, and we'll see if you're up for it."

After classes, we met at the Columbus Circle Train Station, entered, and began the ride home to 103rd Street.

No surprises here, I thought.

I was very surprised, however, when all three of my friends exited the train at the 59th Street and Lexington Avenue station.

"Where are we going?" I asked.

"You'll see," responded Lenny. "Just do what we do if you dare."

Making a beeline for the stairs, my three good friends went directly into the Alexanders Department Store with me in tow. Alexanders was a large store taking up an entire city block on 59th Street and offered everything, from men's furnishings to sporting goods under one roof. But why were we here? What was going on?

I watched them closely touring the store's many aisles and departments when suddenly, and to my amazement, both Steve and Lenny began to place items into their oversized gym bags. With John as their lookout, his neck elongated and ready to announce any salespeople or bystanders approaching. They were packing their school bags with everything, from music cassettes to ties and handkerchiefs. I thought to myself—partly in awe, partly in disgust—this was their after-school activity, stealing! I was flabbergasted, never imagining my three close buddies pilfering items from a store.

A quick escalator ride to the third floor found us in the sporting goods department where the stealing continued and objects, including a baseball glove, were carefully placed in oversized gym bags. I found myself lost in thought, regarding my role in this "caper" and a bit nauseous also as I, too, became a lookout for the trio.

It was then, my head on a swivel looking all around, that I noticed her. She was a seemingly frail elderly woman with gray hair and using a cane to assist her in walking. I would not have noticed her, but I recall seeing her on the first floor as well in our vicinity looking at items and peering about.

Well, no matter, I thought to myself, *she was at least in her sixties and obviously not a "cop."*

Looking back at her, she disappeared into the crowd of shoppers.

After a mind-numbing thirty minutes in the store, Lenny approached me and declared, "Okay, Vic, it's your turn, take something, man, show us you're with us, bro."

Take something, I thought, *Take what? I had never stolen anything in my life, not even small things like chewing gum or potato chips from a bodega, nothing.*

"C'mon," Lenny continued, "you wanted to hang. Do it!" Pointing to a row of men's clothing, he whispered, "Take a shirt, bro! They are easy put it in your bag before anyone sees you"

Walking over to the shirt table, I looked around to see if the "coast was clear" when, once again, I noticed the older lady with the cane, "*La Viejita*," looking at us then veering away quickly. Now was the time, I thought to myself, trying to muster the courage to do the unthinkable and take what did not belong to me. I took the shirt from the table, checking the size, trying to look "normal," then with one swift motion, placed it in my bag. Looking around, I saw no one, meaning I had succeeded in my first theft.

To my delight, I heard John say, "Let's get out of here."

With our school bags filled with ill-gotten items, we made for the exit. As we proceeded toward the Lexington Avenue exit, I felt a sense of relief at our imminent escape and thought to myself that this stealing thing was not for me. I would rejoice with my friends that I had gone along but would never go again. Just as we approached the exit and felt the rush of air from the outside, it happened.

A voice from behind us broke the silence, saying, "Store police, do not move!"

Turning immediately, I saw a large African American man in street clothes with a badge hanging from a chain around his neck, beckoning to the four of us. Also, and to my amazement, there was the little old lady standing next to him, a badge around her neck as well. She was also store security and undercover.

Embarrassingly, we were hustled to a basement room and met by other store detectives who had been "tracking" us since our arrival. To our added astonishment the "elder" woman began to take off her wig and overcoat to reveal what was a "thirtyish" year old, complete with handcuffs and a firearm. She had been in disguise to fool idiot thieves like us, and it worked. We were then asked to empty our gym bags of their contents on a large table, thereby highlighting all of the stolen items.

Our personal information was taken and recorded and we were photographed; our photos to be placed on a "wall of shame" with hundreds of people also caught shoplifting. The lead detective told us that, as juveniles, we were not subject to arrest, but that if we reentered the store, we would be "locked up."

"Will our parents be contacted?" I asked, my voice crackling with fear.

"Not this time," answered the boss. "This is your first offense, but if it happens again, then yes, you will be prosecuted. Now get out of here!"

Going home, nobody spoke; what was there to say? We had been caught by a cop disguised as a little old lady. It was pretty good security if you asked me. After pledging that none of us would tell our parents or anyone else, we parted ways.

Sitting there in my room, I analyzed the events of the day.

I was not a thief, I thought, *and I didn't need a shirt, then why had I almost gotten myself arrested?*

The answer was simple; I, for the third time in my young life, had allowed myself to be "lured or talked into" a dangerous situation by some friends. As I contemplated further, I remembered the words of my guidance counselor at school. He told all of us that this, our junior year, would be the most important of all and colleges would be looking at not only our grades, but our entire record. The idea of my being arrested for shoplifting scared me to my core as his words rang in my head, "Any conviction will not only affect your college admission but will follow you for the rest of your life." Furthermore, he went on to say that this would preclude us from obtaining employment with any government agency and be a "stain" on our lives forever. I sat there for what seemed to be hours, pondering the "break" life had provided me this day and how close I had come to ruining myself.

If, as people say, good things arise from bad, then this was a seminal moment for me. I like to say, even at the risk of sounding melodramatic, that I finally grew up that day and began to think for myself. I did not abandon my lifelong friends, merely found cheerful ways not to be around them so much. Of course, they talked about me behind my back, but who cared as I was on a different path listening to my first instincts and not following anyone.

Sadly, my friend John would succumb to drug and alcohol abuse several years later, another statistic from East Harlem never to see his future.

After the incident, when Mom wanted to shop for me, I always suggested Gimbels or Bloomingdales, never Alexanders. Just saying.

Big Tony to the Rescue (1969)

A violent attack against one of us is an attack on all of us.

Sports were a big part of growing up in East Harlem and New York City during the 1960s and 1970s. I loved both basketball and football with a passion, playing at every opportunity in the various parks in and around the five boroughs. Sports leagues were everywhere throughout the city and the competition was high between clubs from various neighborhoods. At Power Memorial Academy, I played only intramural sports having tried out, unsuccessfully, for the school team. You must understand, Power Memorial was a legendary basketball school having won countless CHSAA Championships throughout the years. They also graduated a young man named Lou Alcindor in 1965 who later went on to become the great Kareem Abdul Jabbar of NBA fame. Still, I enjoyed the competition and became pretty good at both sports.

Saturdays were special as I would go to JHS 117 Park and see the John V. Lindsey Football League games. This two hand touch men's league was comprised of teams from the five boroughs and was extremely competitive with the skill level and inherent violence of most tackle games thereby drawing large crowds of fans weekly. Four games were played each and every Saturday as I rooted for the "Colts," a team comprised of guys from the neighborhood. Their captain and quarterback was a skinny guy nicknamed "Babo," who had led them to numerous championships during the last ten years.

Their blue jerseys with gold trim signified excellence throughout the East Harlem community and I dreamed of playing for them one day.

This Saturday would indeed be a special one as the Colts were playing "the 108th Street Boys," a team comprised of young Italian men whose families had settled in East Harlem in the 1930s and forties and, even with the large Hispanic influx, still called the neighborhood home. Italian Americans still lay claim to several "blocks" in East Harlem predominantly from 108th Street to 116th Street, Second Avenue to the East River, and while the "West Side Story" mentality of the 1950s had dissipated, these boundaries still had to be considered and respected.

It was nine thirty when my close friend, Junie, walked into the 108th Street Park. Junie, an African American, was one of the first guys I had met when I moved here from the Bronx and we stayed "boys." The morning sun shone down on the football field as spectators jockeyed for spots from which to view the contest. Everyone stood for the games, no seating or bleachers. From the Second Avenue entrance, the 108th Street Boys entered, their white jerseys with black numbers glistening. Leading them onto the field was their leader and best player, Big Tony. Tony was a huge man, three hundred pounds or better, but this weight was "poured" over a six-foot-four frame and he carried it with grace and power. Junie and I had posted ourselves near the Second Avenue entrance to better see their entry onto the playing field. It was then that both Junie and I noticed something strange about Tony; he was wearing dress shoes. Tony had a reputation for his Saturday game dress, choosing to sometimes play in the silk pants he had worn the Friday prior, rather than sweats or denim, but always in sneakers.

His teammates could be overheard discussing his footwear when, as if on cue, he suddenly turned, looked directly at me, and said loudly, "Hey, kid, come over here!"

For a moment I stood frozen. *Me*, I thought. *What could Big Tony want with me?*

I had always made it a point to nod at him submissively whenever I passed him on the street, rarely getting a reaction, but so did everyone else in the neighborhood. I had also cheered him on when he caught touchdown passes during games, sometimes drawing the ire of Colt fans.

"You better go ahead, man," whispered Junie, "he's waiting."

"Kid, I need a pair of sneakers fast, can you help me?"

"Yeah!" I said, "The Army and Navy store is open, they have sneakers."

"Great," he grunted, handing me a $50 bill from a wad of money I had only seen in movies. "Size nine and a half and hurry up!"

Without missing a beat, I grabbed the crisp, new bill and, side-kick in tow, sprinted to the Third Avenue store.

I thought about entering the "Tom, Dick, and Harry" Shoe Store for the purchase but stuck to my plan after seeing they were crowded and time was critical; after all, it was Saturday in East Harlem and stores were full. Entering the 107th Street Army and Navy store and completely out of breath from the run, I asked Joe, the owner, for the shoes. Seeing our hurry, he retrieved the Converse box quickly. I also asked him for a pair of sweat socks. Tony had not specified that portion of the purchase, but I inferred he would need them and took a chance; after all, sneakers with nylon dress socks, *ugh!* Tony was too classy for that. Joe had commented on the $50 bill and it being "much too early to break a big bill," but Junie had filled him in on our mission and he tended to us.

"$13.50," he said, handing me the change from the purchase.

I took the money and the receipt counting as I, once again, began sprinting back to the field.

In an instant, we were back in the park going directly to the 108th Street Boys' sideline where I handed Big Tony his order.

Sitting on a bench, he smiled and said, "Hey, this kid's all right, he even got me sweat socks."

This drew laughs from his teammates as the big man put on the socks followed by the high-top Converse sneakers. To everyone's delight, they fit perfectly.

Approaching Tony, I handed him the change from the $50 bill reciting, "Here you go, Tony, your change, $36.50. The receipt is in the bag, sir." I interjected the "sir" as I had been taught to show respect to my elders and I was also standing on a sideline with his thirty-five large teammates. I figured it couldn't hurt.

Without hesitation and not even looking at his change or receipt, Tony motioned me closer to him, his teammates looking on.

"Thanks, kid, you saved my life," he said, adding, "This is for you, take it."

In his colossal hand was a $5 bill, a "tip" for what I had just accomplished. Five bucks in 1969 was a big deal. This was pizza and soda money for both me and Junie with change to spare. A frankfurter for each of us could have also been purchased, with change! We could have really enjoyed that money all day.

To just about everyone's surprise, including myself, I found myself saying, "No, no. Thanks, Tony." The words just came out.

"Why not?" he asked as both he and his teammates looked on in amazement.

"If I took that, then what I did wouldn't have been a favor," I said. "Glad to help, have a great game." With those words, I turned and walked away with Junie in tow, proud of my self-control.

"I can't believe you didn't take the money," whispered Junie, "everybody's still in shock over there." He pointed out.

"It wouldn't have been right, man! It was a favor," I replied.

My father had instilled in me that kindness and helping others was the cornerstone of a good life and forbade me from taking money from people I had helped. He spoke about karma often and that good always comes "back around." I felt good about my actions as we watched the game, cheering Big Tony on.

As always, Big Tony was a force of nature, catching two touchdown passes and excelling in all phases of the contest. To my delight after the win, as he walked off the field, he turned and gave me a wink, pointing to his sneakers.

"That was for you kid!" he said as he departed.

I felt good inside as everyone looked at me in awe.

Breaking me from my stupor, Junie said, "Let's go for pizza, my treat."

As we ate, he reminded me of another "happening" occurring on this day, a basketball game at Benjamin Franklin High School.

The high school was known for hosting games in their huge gymnasium with local teams playing for both trophies and bragging rights. Tonight would be a great contest with none other than the Rucker Park Men's team playing against the King Towers crew.

"It's going to be great!" shouted Junie. "And it's free! Six thirty game time, man. C'mon, let's go."

"How do we navigate 116th Street?" I asked. "How are we going to get home? The game will end around nine o'clock, you going to walk through 116th Street at nine o'clock at night?"

Junie knew exactly what I meant. It was very unwise to tempt fate and walk through 116th Street in the dark of the night. The Redwings were still there. The Redwings, one of the last gangs left in the city, was comprised of tough Italian kids who "claimed" 116th Street as their own. A late-night stroll there would be tempting fate.

We could detour our return home, I thought, *walking uptown to 118th Street and going east to Lexington Avenue but then we chanced the Wagner Projects Crew which also did not like unannounced visitors at night.*

At Junie's urging and bolstered by seeing a great game, we washed up at my house and then set off. Even at six o'clock in the evening, the sun was still shining as we headed north on Third Avenue, shops bristled with business using the sidewalks as their salesrooms. You could buy a variety of things here, from clothing to furniture to food. The Avenue was also home to groups of young ladies traveling together. Us looking at them and them returning smiles, it was glorious. Yet with all this camaraderie swirling around us, I couldn't shake a feeling of foreboding in my bones.

The gym was crowded as was always the case with these games. Skills were on full display as dunks were met with raucous applause as well as *oohs!* and *aahs!* In the end, it was the Rucker team pulling out a hard-earned victory, seventy-two to sixty-nine. Junie had met some of his uptown lady friends and was holding court by the exit.

Pointing to my wrist, I mouthed the words, "Let's go," simultaneously pointing to the windows and impending darkness.

"Relax," he mouthed back as I fidgeted nervously in my seat, but I was no "flat leaver," so I stayed. Cutting out on your friends gave you a negative standing in your social circle.

Finally, Junie finished his rap fest. Displaying a wrinkled piece of loose-leaf paper, he proudly stated, "Got the digits." His way of bragging that one of the young ladies had provided him with her telephone number.

Standing on the top step of the huge stairway in front of Benjamin Franklin High School, we were now both filled with concern. Night had covered El Barrio like a warm blanket and the joyous sounds heard earlier had been replaced by an eerie silence broken only by car horns and street talk peppered with curse words both in Spanish and English.

"Now what?" he whispered. "How are we getting home?"

Surveying the area, our thought patterns similar, we thought about different routes to circumvent unfriendly areas. To my thinking, the best and quickest way home was going directly south, through Jefferson Park. The park ran from 111th Street to 114th Street and First Avenue to the East River Drive and was famous for its huge swimming pool and two football fields. It was still risky but using this route would place us exiting onto 111th Street and only a few blocks from home.

We made a left at the bottom of the stairs and proceeded to walk reaching 114th Street. There, the park greets you with huge trees, assorted shrubbery, and fencing all around. Veering right onto 114th Street, not two minutes into our voyage home, my heart sank. There they were, the Redwings. Gone were the defining sweaters of the 1940s and fifties, but you knew who they were, every East Harlem kid knew. I knew some of them by their nicknames and reputations. There was Crazy Boy, Big Mario, and, worst of all, Billy M... Billy had earned his reputation the street way having visited Spofford, the boy's detention center in the Bronx, on more than one occasion and having participated in several robberies that I knew of; and here he was standing right in front of me. There was nowhere to run. This was their area; nowhere to hide.

"Well, look what we have here!" shouted one of the group. "If it isn't a spic and a nigger just walking through."

Without warning, they were on us. Older guys had told me once that if attacked by a group, try to grab one and beat his butt as you're getting beat. At least you will have gotten one of them. This was not the case here as both Junie and I were being pummeled and kicked from all sides. A punch to the side of my face sent my glasses flying as I hit the cement, the blows reaching their marks. I tried to fight back, but to no avail, as it was nine against two, not good odds in our favor.

As the fight "haze" grew around me, making it impossible to see or hear a voice pierced the night...

"What the hell is going on here?"

I knew that voice, it was indelibly pasted in my mind. It was Big Tony. Through the blood and perspiration, I could make him out as he came out of Rao's Restaurant. Rao's was a very exclusive Italian restaurant located on the corner of 114th Street and Pleasant Avenue, known throughout the city for its food and ambiance. Only the elite and connected got a reservation *ever*.

As my vision returned and wiping away the blood, I saw him clearly. He was resplendent as always in blue sharkskin pants and matching alligator shoes that I saw clearly from my sidewalk vantage point. I recall calling his name in a muffled tone as the gang members relented. His huge hand grabbed my arm and lifted me to my feet as he told the Italian youth not to run, and they didn't.

"What happened?" asked Tony.

"They jumped us for no reason," I replied. "We didn't do anything, Tony, we're just trying to get home," I continued, blood coursing from my split lip.

Junie, also bloodied, remained silent as he knew this was no time for him to speak.

Surprising all, Big Tony handed me his handkerchief saying, "Hey, I know you; you're the sneaker kid from the football game today right!"

"Yeah," I said meekly. "That was me, sir." Once again using the respect Dad taught me.

Imposingly, he approached the gang members, his minions following him ready to attend to his every whim.

"You see this kid!" he shouted. "This kid's a friend of mine. You see him, you leave him alone! He don't bother nobody," he stated loudly.

I remember the looks on the faces of the Redwings as their jaws dropped with surprise and envy.

Then grabbing me by my arm, he pulled me beside him, announcing, "Take a good look at him! You leave him alone!" he repeated aloud. "You mess with him again, we're going to have a problem," Tony said, his voice shattering the night air like a siren. "Why don't you guys give up this whole 'gang' thing?" asked Tony. "I'm going to have to speak to your parents."

The Redwings all nodded and quickly dispersed when told to "Get the hell out of here" by one of Tony's large confederates.

"You all right, kid? Can you make it home?" asked Tony.

"I'll be okay; thanks, Tony," I said, still drying the blood from my mouth with the handkerchief he had provided. "I owe you, Tony," I said in a whisper.

"Nah," he stated, smiling from ear to ear. "Just returning the favor."

Junie and I walked home that evening in complete safety.

East Harlem Heroes (1970)

A hero is any person intent on making this world a better place for all people.

Having just finished several games of three-on-three basketball on the Franklin Plaza court, Herman, Billy, and I had settled into the checkerboard area to rest and take in another sunny Saturday afternoon in El Barrio. People were going about their Saturday tasks with shopping carts and children playing, all reflecting a joyous weekend vibe.

Suddenly, Herman alerted to something that got all of our collective attention. There, in front of my building, stood a family of three and, to our amazement, they were being robbed at knifepoint. Two men stood directly in front of them, menacing them with open knives and relieving them of their valuables. With great quickness, they took two suitcases from the family's hands as well as two thirty-five-millimeter cameras, running away in less than sixty seconds.

"Oh crap!" said Billy. "They're robbing those people."

"Help!" shouted the woman of the group. "They robbed us! Help please," continued her cries, her young daughter weeping openly with fear.

Having taken their bounty, the thieves ran out of the 106th Street entrance toward Third Avenue. Looking at one another quizzically, my friends and I stood there frozen with both fear and indecision. After all, these guys had knives and were brazen enough to accost people in broad daylight. Without a word, however, Herman jumped to his feet and began running in the direction of the fleeing suspects. Asking questions like, "Where the heck are we going?" and "Are you insane, bro?" Billy and I followed, trying to keep up with our brave friend who was now in a full sprint.

Reaching the corner of 106th Street and Third Avenue, the crowds of Saturday shoppers looked at us as we ran by them. Many of them seemed to understand our pursuit, having seen the thieves pass, and motioned and pointed us south on the avenue.

"They went that way," one pedestrian with child in tow whispered, wanting to assist but not get too involved.

As we ran, we could now see the two thieves clearly running two blocks ahead of us, nearing 104th Street across from the Eagle Theater.

"Don't lose them!" shouted Herman, suddenly veering right toward 103rd Street. "I'm going to get Johnny."

Billy and I knew just who he meant. He was getting Johnny R., our boy from 103rd Street. Johnny R. was older than we were and had a reputation for fearing no one having been in the army and many a Harlem skirmish. He would fight when required and detested "dope fiends," as he called them, saying that they were the root of all evil in our neighborhood. The sixties and seventies saw the scourge of heroin decimate the inner cities and we had lost many friends and family to drug abuse. "Junkies," as they were also referred to, would assault and steal to support their addiction.

Billy and I stayed with the thieves as we were now about half a block behind them. They knew they were being followed, looking back periodically while carrying their cumbersome stolen property, suitcases growing ever heavier and cameras swinging back and forth around their tired necks. Once at 102nd Street, we saw them enter the Washington Projects and we immediately knew this was a problem. Billy and I had no friends in this development and had to assume that maybe they did. Were we heading into a trap? Did they have friends here? All good questions without answers yet. To our delight and relief, we were rejoined by Herman and Johnny, both having acquired baseball bats courtesy of John's 103rd Street associates.

Washington Housing Development was teeming with activity on this Saturday afternoon as we entered. To our surprise, there was our quarry standing in the middle of the buildings waiting for us. They had decided to make a stand and stop running, dripping with sweat and obviously out of breath, their addiction getting the better of them. A quick look around reflected no allies or confederates, this was welcome news as the confrontation was about to begin.

"What's you guys problem?" blurted out one of them, knife at the ready.

Their tattered clothing and sallow features validated our suspicions about their drug abuse as did their "nasally" voice tones.

"You know what's up!" Herman fired back. "You guys robbed that family in Franklin, man. They had a kid with them, not cool"

"So!" answered the other lowlife, "What you going to do?"

"We're going to get their stuff back," answered an ever-agitated Johnny, inching his way closer to the target, bat at the ready.

An eerie silence overtook the standoff as both groups pondered their options in the heat of the day.

Will they fight? I thought. *These guys had a good profit coming to them from selling their stolen wares. They were outmatched and outnumbered but clarity of thought was not their best asset right now. They also knew that Johnny and Herman would club them mercilessly before they could use their blades.*

People were starting to mill around us now, inferring from the conversation what had occurred just moments before, another bad omen for the crooks.

"Let us keep something, man!" shouted one of them. "We need to get well," alluding to his drug dependence.

"Give us one of the cameras and a suitcase," said Herman. "C'mon, before we take it all!"

"How do we know you're not going to keep it for yourselves?" replied the other thief, his voice quivering from both fear and heroin withdrawal.

"Because we're not junkies!" replied Johnny angrily, disgusted by the insinuation. "We will give it back to them."

Astonishingly, the thieves dropped one of the suitcases to the ground and placed one of the cameras beside it before walking off, looking back in disgust, seeing their day's profits cut in half. Picking up the stolen items to the faint cheers of dwindling spectators, we walked back to Franklin Plaza our heads held high, having struck a blow for decency, we all thought.

The victimized family was still in front of my building speaking with both Franklin Plaza security and the New York City Police.

"My camera!" shouted the wife, "you got it back, I don't believe it!"

As Herman handed the items to her the husband suddenly and to everyone's amazement, exclaimed, "What about the other stuff?" Apparently disappointed that all his possessions were not recovered.

An angry and frustrated Johnny had to be physically escorted away from the man by me as both the NYPD and neighbors chastised him both for his lack of appreciation and his ignorance as to the workings of the streets.

"Hey," one officer bristled, "do you realize what just happened here? Do you know how fortunate you are to get anything back?"

Unlike him, the man's wife shook our hands, apologizing for her husband's callousness and "stupidity." Surprisingly, their daughter ran up to us, providing heartfelt hugs that lasted several minutes. The hugs and look on her face made the entire adventure worth the danger. Even with the man's lack of pathos and appreciation for our heroic actions, we returned to the checkerboard area happy in the fact that we had done the "right thing" and had protected the "hood" that day.

Insult to Injury/My Dad Dies (1971)

When a great man dies, the light he leaves behind illuminates the paths of other men.

The death of a parent is never easy, no matter the age. My father, Joe Lopez, was a heavy cigarette smoker his entire life, ingesting two to three packs of Winston cigarettes per day. He had been smoking this way since his teenage years and his throat cancer diagnosis, while not surprising to us, still hurt immensely. Cancer is an insidious thing as it affects, not only the person afflicted, but their entire family as round-the-clock care is necessary. My family opted for keeping my father at home for as long as possible which required either my mother or me staying with him to provide much-needed medical and emotional support.

My senior year in high school was supposed to be a wonderful time but with Dad ill, there was no prom or parties; he did, however, muster the strength to attend my graduation and hear my name read as I crossed the stage to receive my diploma. In January of 1970, Joe "Pepe" Lopez died at Calvary Hospital in the Bronx. I was the last to arrive at his bedside and the doctors marveled as to how he "hung on" until I got there. I kissed him on the forehead, told him I loved him, and with that, he was gone. I remember that night was exhausting; my mother and I slept in his bed fully clothed, comforting each other in our grief, knowing that Dad's pain had ended.

The next day arrived and both Mom and I had much to do by way of preparation for my father's viewing. I was given the task of scheduling the funeral mass at our church, Saint Cecilia's, for the upcoming Saturday. My mom had emphasized this date as our family would arrive from Puerto Rico and many other locales for the services. Entering the rectory on 105th Street, I stood in line with folks wishing to schedule weddings, baptisms, and of course, funeral masses. I saw Father Jones in the office and felt confident that I could obtain the date and time I wanted.

"Sorry for your loss, Victor," said Father Jones as I approached the window. "Your dad was a mainstay here and will be missed," he added. "I trust you are here for a funeral mass?"

"Yes," I said, "this coming Saturday please at ten o'clock."

"You're in luck, that date and time are open," he stated. "The cost will be $35, son."

Oh no! I thought, *I had not brought any money with me. Mom had forgotten to give me cash.* "Father," I said, "I don't have the money right now, but I will run home and get it immediately. It will take me ten minutes; could you hold the date and time for me?"

"I can't do that, son" was his reply. "You must pay in cash prior to scheduling; those are church rules."

Bewildered, I looked at the priest stating once again that we needed this date due to family coming.

"You know me, Father Jones," I said. "It will take me no time to return."

"Sorry, son, next in line please" was the cleric's answer as he motioned me to step aside so he could attend another parishioner.

Feelings of anger and resentment raged in me as I ran home. My father, indeed my entire family, had dedicated themselves to this church. Our weekly donations and participation in every "drive" they had such as raffles, Christmas cards, and too many more to name, supported this ministry, and now this betrayal all for $35.

Arriving home, I got the money and, thankfully, the date and time were still available when I returned. Handing him the money, I said nothing, but he knew by my silence that he had hurt me and my family and that this would not be soon forgotten. On the walk home, it was my father's words that rang in my brain. He had always spoken to me about the power of money and how greed could ruin everything from friendships to marriages. His famous adage was, "Friends, a friend is a dollar in your pocket," and now, even in death, his words rang true. His church, for which he worked tirelessly for, would not provide him with a mass unless the money was paid in advance. Even as a true Catholic and believer, I never viewed the church in quite the same light after that day. Don't get me wrong, I still attended church and believed in the power of prayer, but that childlike way of looking at organized religion was gone.

My emotions were in a flurry as I arrived back home this important day to continue to assist my mother with the funeral arrangements for my father. Entering the apartment, I was surprised to see two men in the living room talking with Mom. These two men, clad in business suits, shook my hand and introduced themselves as representatives from the Wakefield Monument Company. They stated that they provided "the finest gravestones throughout the five boroughs" as one of them handed me a business card. The other man was asking my mother questions about my father and simultaneously sketching a rendition of what Dad's headstone could look like. He wanted to know my fathers or families patron saint and favorite saying and also inquired about colors and other personal things. All in all, they seemed knowledgeable and very professional and came up with an excellent rendering of what a perfect headstone for Dad would be bringing my poor mother to tears when she saw it.

"The entire cost will be $420, Mrs. Lopez," said the man identifying himself as Mr. E. Rome. "A 50 percent down payment can get work started immediately."

Mom went to her bedroom and emerged with $200 in ten- and twenty-dollar bills, asking, "When will it be placed in the cemetery?"

"In about four weeks," responded the salesperson as he handed me a receipt.

After the two men left, Mom said she was going to the funeral parlor to finish making arrangements. I opted to stay home as both events this day had sapped my strength.

Mary Lopez returned to her home an hour later, teary-eyed and obviously exhausted. It seemed that the funeral director stated to her that my father would require a closed casket because of the facial deformities caused by his oral cancer. This meant my extended family would not be able to say a proper goodbye to their patriarch. Crushing! The funeral for Joe Lopez was beautiful as funerals go. Dad was adored by all because he was always there when people needed him. The funeral mass was also well done and Father Jones seemed especially attentive and comforting. I smiled at him several times and knew now that he was just following church protocol and that Dad meant a lot to him. My anger had been erased by the caring shown to my family by this gracious man. I was wrong to expect a special treatment that day and have hateful feelings in my heart. I would confess my shortcomings as soon as I could. Lessons learned.

We laid my father to rest that morning. We knew the headstone would not be ready for a while and that was okay with everyone. Four weeks passed and my mother had diligently called the monument company weekly, inquiring about our purchase. At first, a woman's voice answered, saying that the stone would be "delayed" for some reason or another then, at six weeks, no one answered her calls. We all knew something was wrong. My uncle contacted the Bronx Police and our worst suspicions were confirmed, we had been scammed!

The Wakefield Monument Company did not exist and these two men had been ripping people off for two years, preying on people when they were their most vulnerable after the death of a loved one. In hindsight, I could see it clearly, as hindsight always is. How did they know our address and that my father had even died? The police later confirmed that they had a confederate working at the hospital that was providing them with information on the recently deceased for a price. Some of my family members went to the address on the receipt, only to find a vacant lot. We also found out that these jerks had cheated some families out of thousands of dollars, promising to build them mausoleums and keeping the down payments. A year passed and my father's gravestone was still unmarked when we received a call from the Bronx district attorney's office, saying that Mr. Rome was in police custody. Apparently, he turned himself into the authorities after learning that many people were looking to do him harm because of his actions. My family was then contacted by a legitimate company that was offering discounts to the families that had been tricked by this con artist who, after all this time and in a fit of self-preservation, made restitution to all the people he had scammed.

On March 1, 1971, thirteen months after his death, Joe Lopez finally had a headstone honoring him at Saint Raymond's Cemetery. That day when we went to finally pay proper respects to him, I heard his words, once again, echoing in my head. I had been angry at both the Catholic church and the scum who took advantage of me and my mother, but, as Dad would say, "You cannot let anger consume you, my son; when you do, the enemy wins, not you."

I stood there praying with my mother and finally said a teary goodbye to Dad, touching his beautiful headstone repeatedly and thinking that, in this world, one must always be careful and cautious, even in death.

The Attack of the Half Man (1972)

Never underestimate anyone; you do so at your own peril.

Having completed my sophomore year at Fordham University, my mom and I had begun to heal from my father's death from throat cancer the year before. Things steadily improved and I began working part-time at a Third Avenue men's shop to earn some extra bucks; 1972 was also the year I had also been introduced to the world of salsa music and dancing and couldn't get enough. Like so many others, I spent hours practicing my "moves" in front of my mom's living room mirror, listening to records played on the combination record player, radio, and television cabinet. This piece of furniture would be ours after just a few more monthly payments. Here I was, practicing my dance steps to my Joe Cuba album, my mother providing me timely tips as she was a good dancer in her day.

I began to go out on Friday or Saturday nights. The seventies and salsa craze had produced many dance clubs throughout the five boroughs. Not only could you dance at Manhattan clubs like the Cheetah and the Corso, but the outer boroughs like the Bronx and Queens were also packing people in to hear this dance music pioneered by Willie Colon and Johnny Pacheco to name but a few.

This particular evening, I was headed to the Royals II, located on Castle Hill Avenue in the East Bronx. I was also excited because my Uncle Tony had lent me his car, a 1969 Impala, even above the objections of my mother. As always, my clothes were pressed and ready and at ten o'clock in the evening, I set out to the club. The drive from East Harlem to the Bronx was quick and I was fortunate to find a parking spot a few doors down from the club's entrance. Staring at my watch, it was now ten thirty, still too early to go in. In the rearview mirror, I could see people paying the five-dollar cover charge to enter and I could see Benny at the door. Good old Benny. He had grown up in El Barrio two blocks from where I had, on 107th Street and Lexington Avenue. Benny had been a member of the Targeteers Street gang growing up and was older than me, but he always said hi to me and looked out for me and others on the block. Big Benny, as he was known, was a large man, not tall, but with a large frame and massive arms. His trademark, "bear hug," was his signature move and if he locked arms around you, it was over and you eventually gave up. I understood why the club owners put him out front every evening as he knew how to both deescalate situations and address trouble expeditiously when it arose.

Gazing at my Timex, exactly one-half hour had passed and it was time to go in and dance a bit. During my wait, I had noticed a man in a wheelchair panhandling near the club entrance. Growing up in New York and other cities, you are taught to keep your head "on a swivel," looking out for trouble, and even in a locked car, I was still cognizant of my surroundings. Yet *a guy in a wheelchair*, I thought, *no threat, no problem.*

As I opened the car door, I discovered that the wheelchair was no longer several feet away but directly in front of me along with its occupant, a half man. This person in the chair had no legs. His body consisted of an upper torso with nothing but thigh "remnants" or stubs below the waist. As we locked eyes, I knew I had seen him before, and then it came to me. This was the same guy who begged for money on the subway. On the train, he used a "box" with wheels to go from car to car, soliciting money from riders. I recall him being very nasty to people who did not give him their change, and here he was, staring me in the face. I could see that the upper body he did have was huge with large shoulders and biceps accrued from years of wheelchair manipulation, no doubt. On both hands, he wore work gloves, once again to help him propel his chair and avoid injury.

"Let me get a dollar!" he shouted as I closed and locked the car door, still blithely unaware of the imminent danger I was in.

Overcoming my surprise at this request, I replied, "Sorry, bro, I ain't got no dollar." Attempting to sound as "street" as I possibly could.

Without so much as another word, this "half man" leaped on me, grabbing me by my jacket lapels. I, in reflex, also grabbed him by his shirt, pulling him out of his chair. Now inner-city training always dictated that you do not allow anyone in your space. I had seen many guys get "sucker" punched while talking and allowing a foe to get too close, but this was different; who would think a disabled guy would attack?

As our struggle continued, I could feel his leg "stubs" around my midsection. *Ugh!* I drew back my right fist and delivered a punch with all my might directly to his face that had no reaction whatsoever. Trying to break his viselike grip, we struggled to and fro, clanging against a store gate, the sound resonating into the night air. I hurled two more solid blows at his face, but he did not even flinch. He had a "crazed" look in his eyes and reeked of alcohol, which probably added to his superior strength and recklessness. Then it came to me what this attacker was trying to achieve. He was doing his best to topple me off my feet. If he succeeded in knocking me down, he would have a clear advantage and I would be at his mercy. Trying to react quickly, I spread my legs, thereby widening my fighting stance. This would provide me more balance. We grappled for what seemed like forever when suddenly, a tremendous "*BOOM!*" broke the night air. My assailant immediately broke his grip on me, falling to the asphalt. As I turned to where the sound had come from, there was Benny at the club entrance, a .38 caliber Smith and Wesson pistol in his hand. He had fired a shot into the air to ward off the thug. Dazed with my forehead cut and bleeding, I ran toward the club entrance, turning to see my attacker jump into his wheelchair and speed away. He was almost near the corner now, pushing his wheels with extreme force in order to make his escape. Benny grabbed my arm and assisted me as I was obviously about to pass out. Other club personnel and guests flooded the entrance as I was escorted inside and given aid for my bleeding.

"What happened?" was the question presented by several customers as they witnessed my condition. I looked at Benny praying that he would not reveal every detail of the assault as the embarrassment would be mortifying.

Looking at me with that wonderful Benny smile, he replied to them, "Some guys tried to rob Vic, but he fought them off."

This response was met with applause and pats on my back. The owner offered me free entry for my next visit and even though I was too young, various people attempted to purchase drinks for me all evening when they heard of my "bravery." Several ladies introduced themselves, lauding my valor and asking me to dance.

As the evening wore on, Big Benny filled me in on my assailant, saying that he was indeed a "bad seed" and was known throughout the neighborhood as a goon and a thief. He also chastised me for not paying enough attention to my surroundings.

"You never know where evil is coming from," he said.

It was then that I thanked him for his discretion regarding my attacker.

In pure "Benny" fashion, he replied, whispering in my ear, "What was I supposed to tell folks, my man, that you got attacked by half a dude?"

We both laughed the rest of the night away and I learned from then on never to underestimate anyone.

OX and The Bronx Bombers 1972

"Courage doesn't mean you don't fear, it means you don't let fear stop you"

1972 was a great year for me. Among other things it was the year I was given a "spot" or playing position, on the Colts Football team. The Colts football team were the champions of the John V. Lindsey East Harlem Football League whose two hand touch games were played on the cement of 109 th Street Park in East Harlem every Saturday during the fall. I had wanted to play for them for as long as I can remember, having tried out twice before being cut, but I had both practiced and grown since then and was now part of the team, a rookie. Working hard and attending practices I knew the position I wanted to play, center and long snapper. Marty, the current snapper, was getting on in years and I knew they were looking for a replacement. I "hiked' the ball well in practice and familiarized myself with all the plays, drawing the attention of the veteran players who told me to be "ready" when my time came.

It was now October and five games into the season, and I still had not played. We were 5 and 0 and had the best record in the league yet I began to doubt myself and thoughts of quitting were surfacing in my mind, but I stayed on hoping for an opportunity to show what I could do. Little did I know that that day would arrive sooner than I would have imagined.

Game 6 was upon us already and the crisp autumn air was filled with anticipation in El Barrio. This was the day the Colts were scheduled to play their arch enemies, The Bronx Bombers and their captain and defensive stalwart, Ox. Ox, as he was affectionately known, was their scary 6'3, 240-pound defensive tackle who struck fear into opposing offensive lineman. With his long, flowing hair cascading around his gnarled face, he was an ominous sight to behold. This imagery was further enhanced by the fact that he always played in combat boots, never sneakers, and was always scowling and seemed erratic in nature no doubt to instill fear in his opponents, successfully, I might add. From my past observations and close study of his games, I had gained insight into his most valuable weapons, his forearms. Ox had perfected the habit of wrapping his forearms with white surgical tape. This practice was not uncommon among both offensive and defensive lineman during the 1970's. However, in his case he used so much of the stuff that it formed "cast- like" guards on both his forearms that he used to inflict punishment on offensive lineman throughout the game. This practice had been brought up at league meetings and should have been banned, but to no avail. Ox continued striking out with these illegal weapons, pummeling linemen who attempted to block him, causing bloody broken noses and other gory facial lacerations.

At exactly nine o'clock the whistle blew, signifying it was game-time and the conflict was about to begin. My nerves were on edge despite my outward bravado. I knew that Marty had been nursing several injuries, but I secretly hoped that he would last this game as I did not want my first Colt's game to be against this madman and face possible injury. The first half saw two great football teams locked in a defensive struggle with very few productive offensive plays ending in a 6 to 6 tie. Several skirmishes had broken out during the first half as there was also a general dislike and bad blood between the two teams. Of course, Ox and his illegal onslaught with his contrived forearm weaponry continued, having once again, drawn blood, from one of our players. The referees were again made aware of this and, once again, stated that this was a "league" issue not one for field judgements. We watched as this drew smirks from the cretons on the opposite team. Finally, the whistle blew signifying halftime and both teams returned to their respective sidelines for rest and strategy meetings. As I stood there among the entire Colts team, I saw Marty walking towards me, and I knew it was that time. He stated abruptly and almost apologetically, "I can't go anymore kid, you have to take my spot this half, are you ready?" His words reverberated in my brain and caused me to shiver a bit yet, trying to stay composed among my teammates, I exclaimed in my gruffest voice, "Hell Yeah, I am ready, Let's go"! This of course was met with loud yells and hoots from my fellow players hoping to instill confidence in me and the entire team.

The next twenty minutes were a blur with Marty and the other offensive lineman providing me tips on how to block the savage I was about to encounter. "Keep your head up when you hike the ball" said our 6'8 guard Teddy, "he likes to get under your chin with that forearm". I said little during this tutorial and was glad that what was said meshed with my prior observations of Ox's playing regimen. "Keep him in front of you", added our all-star tackle Macho Valdez. "If he gets by you, he'll surely try to hurt Babo". Babo was our star quarterback, and I understood the gravity of the fact that any injury to him meant a loss, not only today, but for the rest of the season. As they spoke, I tried to internalize all their ideas while trying to hide my intense fear and trepidation. It felt good that the entire team was pulling for me but looking across the field directly at my immense opponent I knew that it was solely up to me to perform.

My thoughts were shattered by the shrill sound of the whistle signifying the start of the second half. We were set to receive this half so out onto the field I strode, my first game as a Colt. After our reception on the twenty-yard line we huddled up for Babo's play call. As he spoke, I felt ten sets of eyes staring at me causing me to respond adamantly, "Hey guys, let's do this! I am ready"! This seemed to calm all players down and drew smiles from the veterans. "Run right on two", blurted Babo. "Run right on two", he repeated. "Ready Break!" was the answer blurted out by ten men clapping in unison.

Jogging up to the line of scrimmage I saw him standing directly in front of me. He had positioned himself right over the center. "Oh man", he shouted, "fresh meat", let's see what you got rookie," he continued his tirade shouting for all to hear. This caused his fellow players to, once again smirk, and even laugh out loud. As he took his stance right in front of me, I could hear him breathing heavily like some farm animal. Of course, I knew all this was designed to break my concentration and fluster me," it wasn't going to happen", I thought to myself. "Remember the count", I thought to myself repeatedly. "On two", I reminded myself trying hard to memorize the snap count and put away all distractions. Then Babo's voice came clear in my head, no outside noise, no crowd sounds, just his cadence as I had heard it years before as a spectator. "Team down, Ready Set, Signals On, Hut one Hut two". At the sound of 'two', I hiked a perfect ball to our quarterbacks' hands and felt a sense of relief. This sensation would not last long. As I went to block Ox, I felt a crushing blow under my chin. I had concentrated so much on getting the hike right I had forgotten my positioning and allowed him access to my chin with that forearm he used so well. I managed to keep him in front of me with some assistance from my right guard Macho, but the pain was intense. His blow had also struck me partially in the throat disrupting both my breathing and my ability to swallow. The play resulted in a nominal gain and returning to our huddle I did my best to disguise my anguish from my teammates. It was in our huddle that I felt a "gravel" like substance on my tongue and on my lips. Macho looked at me and after examining my open mouth declared, "your tooth is broken bro, welcome to the league". This announcement was met with laughter and pats on my shoulder which bolstered me to hide my despair and keep on playing.

Babo's voice rang out again in our huddle. "Pass play to Danny, pass play to Danny, give me some time kid," our leader said, looking directly at me." Keep Ox off me". I nodded as he spoke. "On one, On one.

"Ready Break"! resounded once again as ten men clapped with one goal in mind and walked to meet their adversaries. "How's your mouth kid?" "Gunna quit yet"? Asked Ox in his most mocking way. Saying nothing I glared at him with new disdain and hatred but remained composed taking deep breaths and trying to concentrate. I remembered the words of my High School coach when he would say to us not to let anyone "get under your skin "as anger convoluted. At "Hut one" the ball was, once again, perfectly given to my quarterback with both speed and precision. Unlike the prior play, this time I was ready for Ox's onslaught with knees bent, head up, and my weight properly distributed. Now it was I who delivered the first blow striking him violently directly in the sternum. Feeling his forward progress slow due to the blow, I engaged him one on one pushing him with all my might and driving him with my legs. I also managed to grab his jersey a bit and hold on, unbeknownst to the referees as this provided me with more leverage. To my delight and his utter surprise this move caused him to lose his balance, toppling him to the asphalt. I hovered over him, as I had been taught to do, making sure he would not arise this play to cause more havoc. I reveled in the look of astonishment on his face and that of his teammates as he lay prone on the cement. Adding insult to the moment Babo had managed to throw a perfect pass to Danny and we went ahead by a touchdown. After a successful extra point attempt that brought the score to 13-6, I was met with thundering applause by my sideline as we came off the field. I felt relieved as I had proven my worth this day against a monstrous adversary and the fear that accompanied the unknown.

The rest of the game was a continued battle in the football "trenches" with Ox, having been embarrassed by the rookie, continuing to try and "club" me and me going directly at his mid-section instead of waiting to be hit. This turned out to be an excellent strategy as the Colts beat the Bronx Bombers that day by a score of 13-6 and remained in first place. Fortunately, I did not suffer any further injuries at the hands of this madman as I now understood his tactics and remained vigilant.

After the game, the revelry continued with the veterans lauding me for my efforts and reliving the play when suddenly the situation changed drastically. Several of my older teammates encircled me in what can only be described as a protective circle. When I asked what was happening one of them pointed to a man crossing the field of play, it was Ox. Apparently, Ox had also been known as a sore loser who, at times, would pick a fight with opposing players if things had not gone his way, and here he was coming straight at me." Don't worry kid" said Teddy, his massive body looming over me, "We got your back". My heart sank with fear as I saw this hulking man drawing ever closer to me his white jersey stained and spattered with blood and still wearing his forearm casts." What would he do?" I thought. I had gotten the best of him fair and square, but this was not the NFL, this was what was considered "street ball" and anything could happen.

I felt my teammates tighten their circle around me as Ox arrived on our sideline. "Hey"! he shouted," why so tense"? apparently feeling the emotion and protective aura." I just came over to congratulate the rookie on a good game. I haven't been clocked like that in a while". With that he extended his huge right hand towards me. "See you next time kid, be ready for another war". I shook his hand losing mine in his viselike grip. "Thanks", I said. "I'll be ready for you". This retort drew a smile from my opponent as he calmly walked back to his sideline. I stayed at the park that day watching the other games and happily receiving the accolades from those players who had witnessed my performance. I do not know what felt better, winning at football, or the battle over fear. Mom took me to the dentist the following Monday.

Salsa Night at the Cheetah/ Dance Injury 1973

"There are shortcuts to happiness and dancing is one of them"

In 1973 New York, and the world, was transfixed by an innovative mixture of Latin beats, rhythms and vocal accompaniment now known as Salsa. This new Latin dance music introduced by Johnny Pacheco, Jerry Masucci and the newly formed Fania Record Company, had exploded onto the dance scene and had given rise to clubs now featuring Latin recording artists and Salsa events. Famous and well-established New York venues such as the Copacabana and the El Morocco, that formerly would not cater to Latin events, now found themselves clamoring to hire Latin dance bands and cash in on this new craze,with some even featuring Salsa Nights and other promotions. I found myself going "dancing" two maybe three times a week to clubs throughout the five boroughs, while still concentrating on my Fordham University school work, keeping my scholarship and attending all my classes.

I had two close friends who began to share my love of Salsa music and the Mambo craze. Together, my friends Kevin, Juan and I would practice our moves for hours in my house on 106 th Street in front of my mother's huge living room mirror. This vintage mirror had been in her family for generations, and it served our practice sessions well as we were able to critique our styles and especially our turns. Turns were an integral part of Salsa dancing and had to be done with care and skill. This Saturday evening, we found ourselves, once again, practicing in front of my mom's mirror before going out. Juan and I had become quite adept at our dancing and had also added some new turns to our repertoire and our confidence was rising. Our friend Kevin however was still a bit "raw". "Don't be so stiff", Juan would say to him as he tried, in vain, to" loosen him up". "You have to move your hips more", I chimed in, but he was still a work in progress. "I want to learn the turns'; Kevin would always say during our practice sessions. "You guys are turning, and I'm still stuck with the basics" he would scream in both frustration and anger. "You can't turn yet bro", Juan would yell back." Only when your basic steps are mastered can you add the turns" he would preach with Kevin only getting more and more discouraged.

It was 10:00 p.m. as we boarded the Number 6 Lexington Avenue train downtown heading for Broadway and 53rd Street and the famous Cheetah Club. This was another landmark New York City night spot that now featured Latin events.

Just two years prior in 1971 the Fania All Stars had first performed live at the Cheetah officially ushering in and introducing the world to the sounds of Salsa music. There was also a best-selling Latin album and a movie "Our Latin Thing" that were offshoots of this live event. We exited the train at 51 Street and headed to the west side at a vigorous pace. It was now 10:30 and we hoped to be on the dance floor by 11:00 p.m. a good time to arrive being neither early nor late. The line outside the club was already forming but we managed to secure a spot and paid our $5.00 entry fee. Once inside we marveled at the place with its strobe lighting and immense dance floor. This night we would be listening to the Willie Colon band complete with their star lead singer, Hector Lavoe. They were already setting up on stage, so we began our usual practice of "scoping" out the ladies on the floor. Of the three of us, Juan was the most outspoken and never missed an opportunity to converse with the opposite sex. He was ruggedly handsome and was more confident than both Kevin and I and usually served as the "icebreaker" of the trio. This would be true this evening as well when, without so much as a warning, he began to speak to a group of young women standing directly in front of us.

"Good evening, ladies", I heard him utter in a contrived, almost baritone voice used, no doubt, to project a more worldly persona. "My name is Juan; these are my boys Kevin and Vic". We both nodded politely and after their initial girly laughter, these ladies responded with heartfelt hellos and began introducing themselves to us. "Yes!" I thought, Juan had done it again.

Now, amid the clamor of the huge crowd with its conversations and white noise I heard a familiar, unmistakable voice, I knew that sound and turning towards the stage I could see its origin. There was Mr. Willie Colon, his hands clasped together saying in a melodious tone "one, two; one, two, three, four" and with that his band sprang to life. Energy began to flow from the huge crowd of dancers as the music encompassed the entire room and couples began to sway to the rhythms of this intoxicating music. With that Juan extended his hand towards one of our new female friends and she gladly accepted his offer to dance. Making eye contact with her friend I too extended my hand asking her to dance and happily my offer also was accepted. Glancing over at Kevin I could see that he was hesitant but surprisingly, he also extended his hand to one of the ladies and was also met with a resounding "yes". "Excellent", I thought we had all broken the "ice" simultaneously and found willing dance partners.

The dance floor was a wondrous thing of beauty as countless couples displayed their moves pulsating to the sounds of clave and bongo. My partner followed my lead well and I smiled at her receiving a cute grin in return. "Always look at your partner," I remember my older friend Roberto telling me over and over as he shared his dancing expertise with me. "You must be in sync with your partner and become one with the music". At the time I thought this advice was a bit much but turns out Roberto was correct. Attention to the lady with whom you were dancing made you a stronger, more confident dancer. I was now glad to have heeded his advice as I was succeeding this evening. Glancing over the crowded floor I could see that Juan was also doing well, smiling and completing turns we had practiced, but where was Kevin? In all the crowding and constant movement, I had lost sight of my friend and his new partner. This was not unusual in a large dance club as the crowd, coupled with all that gyration, sometimes caused you to "drift" on the floor ending up far from where you began. I hoped Kevin had listened to our advice that evening. We had spoken about him "keeping it simple and not attempting any difficult turns". Roberto had also covered this topic with us saying that it was better to do the simple stuff well, than attempt the more difficult moves and fail. This advice still resonated in my head as I had seen firsthand some guys try advanced turns and moves and fail miserably some suffering terrible embarrassment.

Trying to stay positive I concentrated on my partner. Upon closer examination I could see she was more accomplished than I was and had mastered many difficult steps, but she was enjoying my lead by following me closely and smiling with approval. Suddenly my joy came to an abrupt halt! In the distance, and above the din, a woman's painful cry could be heard. This harrowing shriek was quickly followed by continuous moans coming from somewhere on the dance floor. Couples next to us, also hearing these horrific sounds, stopped their dancing in their tracks looking for the root of the screams. I attempted to continue dancing but my partner stopped immediately and began to walk, with me in tow, towards the middle of the floor. As we approached the now large group of bystanders in mid floor my dance partner also let out a loud scream. There, hunched over in what seemed to be excruciating pain, was one of the girls in her group clutching her left arm. In an instant it dawned on me that this was the young lady that Kevin had asked to dance and now she was in terrible pain and begging for assistance. Club security responded quickly as the young woman's friends had now encircled her. Juan and his partner soon arrived and, as our eyes met, he motioned for me to follow him away from the scene. As we moved slowly away, we overheard onlookers whispering the same questions. "What happened to her?"" Did she fall?" "Was she stepped on?" All valid dance club questions as many things can occur on extremely crowded dance floors. Salsa moves, often combined with alcohol consumption, occasionally led to foot injuries and indeed fisticuffs on the floor, but these instances were rare. Most often dancers would apologize for stepping on you and keep going. As we saw the young lady being led off the floor Juan turned to me and said what we were both thinking. "You think

Kevin is responsible for this"? "Where is he"? "I don't know bro but that is the girl he was dancing with, right?' "Yes, it was, "Juan replied, keeping his voice at a whisper as we continued covertly to distance ourselves from the chaotic scene.

Having moved sufficiently far from the action we were still within earshot of the goings on and could still hear the poor young woman's distress. Emergency Medical Personnel had arrived at the club entrance and found it necessary to place her arm and shoulder in a sling for support. They then walked her to a waiting ambulance. We then overheard her friends state loudly that they would meet her at Lenox Hill Hospital. As things slowly began to normalize, Juan and I were astonished to see our two former dance partners approaching us in an aggressive manner. Defensively, but with concern, Juan asked, "What happened? Is she OK?" "NO, she is not OK!" was the resounding answer from both parties. "Her arm may be broken!" said my former partner." Apparently, your friend tried to do a fancy inverted dance turn and almost crippled her". Juan and I looked on in astonishment as she regaled us with the story but, we both instinctively knew what had happened. Kevin had tried an extremely difficult, behind the back, inverted turn and had accidently pulled up on the young lady's arm when it was behind her. This turned a dancing move into one that could only be compared to a wrestling or police maneuver causing agonizing pain and injury. "You want to know the worst part?" my angry ex-partner screamed drawing the attention of several patrons, "the coward just left her there in pain, my friend says she saw him run away and leave the club".

Juan and I stood there in disbelief, not at the fact that Kevin had attempted this ill-conceived dance move, but that he would choose to run away and leave this poor young woman. "When you see your boy tell him that he sucks as a person" the young lady screamed for all to hear as she and her friend departed.

As we walked around the huge venue, we could feel eyes peering at us in judgement. People were whispering and some even pointed fingers. Finally, we determined that staying at the club would not be an option that evening as we were quickly labeled co-conspirators in the maiming of the young lady. Exiting the club, we headed for the train and home. We sat on an Uptown number 6 train aghast at the evening's occurrences. How could such a promise filled evening go so wrong, so quickly? "I told him not to try those turns," said Juan. "And to just run away"' I chimed in, "What was he thinking?' "I guess he just panicked", added Juan as the train barreled us home to 103rd street.

The next day was a basketball day and we met Kevin in White Park eager to hear his take on the night's catastrophe. He said the dancing was going "really well" and as it went on his confidence began to grow. "Looking around I saw other couples doing these great turns and I decided to go ahead and try", big mistake Huh!"

"Yeah"! We added. He stated that he had gotten as far as placing the girls arm behind her when "it got stuck" and he couldn't recover, he then made the fatal mistake of pulling up on the arm thereby causing the "accident". "You should have just turned her loose", I said. "That would have been embarrassing", Kevin replied. "More embarrassing than almost crippling someone", I said tersely. "Anyway", he continued," when she screamed, I panicked and just ran to the nearest exit", I even took a cab home. I feel terrible", he added "I didn't sleep all night". "Was she OK?" he asked meekly. "Hell no"! we both answered. As we told him of the events that followed his early departure you could see that Kevin was remorseful and despondent. We had all been raised to do no harm to our fellow man and this was weighing heavily on him. "I hope her arm wasn't broken", he said. Trying to assuage his broken spirit I answered that I thought it may only have been a sprain.

"Don't tell anybody about this, please!" Kevin pleaded with us, and that day we promised never to reveal what had occurred that evening. It took Kevin several months to get over his dancing debacle as he didn't venture out clubbing with us for a long time. He eventually did return to salsa dancing but only attempting the basics, keeping the turns at a minimum and never returning to The Cheetah Club again. Juan and I came up with our own dancing slang and often said to each other, "be careful with your turning, don't get caught up in a Kevin". When told of this, Kevin didn't find it funny at all. Que Viva La Salsa!

About the Author

Victor López was born in the Bronx, New York, but raised in the Manhattan neighborhood known as East Harlem or "El Barrio." As a teacher in 1976, he rose through the ranks in education shifting from a teacher of social studies and choral music to director of the Harbor School for Performing Arts before becoming Principal of PS/MS 96, all located in his beloved neighborhood of El Barrio. Through his work in education spanning over forty years and a belief that all students can succeed no matter what their economic background or home life is, Mr. Lopez pushed his students to be great. Mr. Lopez has consulted with school districts in many states and internationally grooming both teachers and administrators to teach students and not their circumstances. Mr. Lopez went on to become a founding member of the educational consulting group, Educators for Student Success, where he empowered New York City principals to bring their very best to their classrooms and strive to improve school effectiveness for all school stakeholders. Mr. Lopez continues to work tirelessly to foster the concepts of cultural pride and family values among the younger generation of today.

CPSIA information can be obtained
at www.ICGtesting.com
Printed in the USA
LVHW050421180122
708477LV00020B/892

9 781662 458088